Unbeatable Year 5 SPaG practice from CGP!

The best way for pupils to improve their Grammar, Punctuation and Spelling in Year 5 (ages 9-10) is by doing as much practice as they can.

That's where this book comes in. It's packed with questions that'll test them on all the crucial Grammar, Punctuation and Spelling skills, including those introduced for the first time in Year 5.

And there's more! Everything is perfectly matched to the National Curriculum and we've included answers at the back. Enjoy!

What CGP is all about

Our sole aim here at CGP is to produce the highest quality books — carefully written, immaculately presented and dangerously close to being funny.

Then we work our socks off to get them out to you — at the cheapest possible prices.

Contents

Grammar

Section 1 – Word Types

Nouns 4
Verbs 5
Modal Verbs 6
Adjectives 8
Adverbs 9
Pronouns 12
Relative Pronouns 13
Determiners 14

Section 2 – Clauses and Phrases

Clauses 15
Basic Relative Clauses 16
Trickier Relative Clauses 18
Phrases 20

Section 3 – Conjunctions and Prepositions

Co-ordinating Conjunctions............. 21
Subordinating Conjunctions 22
Using Conjunctions for Cohesion ... 23
Prepositions 24

Section 4 – Linking Ideas

Linking Ideas in a Paragraph 26
Linking Paragraphs 28

Section 5 – Verb Tenses

Present Tense and Past Tense........ 30
Verbs with 'ing' 31
The Present Perfect 32

Section 6 – Standard and Non-Standard English

Standard and Non-Standard English 33

Punctuation

Section 7 – Sentence Punctuation

Capital Letters and Full Stops..................... 36
Question Marks 37
Exclamation Marks 38
Sentence Practice 39

Section 8 – Commas

Commas in Lists 40
Commas to Avoid Confusion 42
Commas After Subordinate Clauses........... 44
Commas After Fronted Adverbials 46
Commas for Extra Information 48
Comma Practice 50

Section 9 – Brackets and Dashes

Brackets for Extra Information 52
Dashes for Extra Information..................... 54

Section 10 – Apostrophes

Apostrophes for Missing Letters 56
Apostrophes for Single Possession............ 57
Apostrophes for Plural Possession 58
Its and It's 59
Apostrophe Practice 60

Section 11 – Inverted Commas

Punctuating Speech.................................... 62
Punctuating Speech in Two Parts 64

Section 12 – Paragraphs and Layout

Paragraphs... 65
Headings and Subheadings 67

Contents

Spelling

Section 13 – Prefixes

Prefixes — 'under', 'over', 'en' and 'em' 68
Prefixes — 'mid', 'pre', 'fore' and 'non'.......70
Hyphenating Prefixes 72

Section 14 – Word Endings and Suffixes

Word Endings — The 'shun' Sound 74
Word Endings — The 'shus' Sound 76
Word Endings — The 'shul' Sound 77
Word Endings — 'ant' and 'ent' 78
Word Endings — 'ance', 'ancy'
 and 'ence', 'ency' 80
Word Endings — 'able', 'ible',
 'ably' and 'ibly' 82
Suffixes..84

Section 15 – Confusing Words

'ei' and 'ie' Words 86
Words with 'ough' in................................88
Words with Silent Letters 90
Unstressed Vowels 92
Homophones 94

Section 16 – Mixed Spelling Practice

Mixed Spelling Practice 96

Glossary...99
Answers 101

Published by CGP

Editors
Keith Blackhall, Heather Cowley, Emma Duffee, Catherine Heygate, Gabrielle Richardson, Sam Summers
With thanks to Andy Cashmore for the proofreading.

ISBN: 978 1 78294 133 0

Clipart from Corel®
Printed by Elanders Ltd, Newcastle upon Tyne.
Based on the classic CGP style created by Richard Parsons.

Text, design, layout and original illustrations © Coordination Group Publications Ltd. (CGP) 2022
All rights reserved.

Photocopying this book is not permitted, even if you have a CLA licence.
Extra copies are available from CGP with next day delivery • 0800 1712 712 • www.cgpbooks.co.uk

Section 1 — Word Types

Nouns

Nouns are words that **name things**.

Concrete nouns are names for things that you can **see**, **touch**, **smell** or **hear**. → chair   road   owl

happiness   power   success ← **Abstract nouns** are names for **ideas** or **feelings**.

Collective nouns are names for **groups** of people or things.

a **pack** of wolves   a **gang** of thieves   a **gaggle** of geese

1 **Write the nouns below next to the correct heading.**

house   swarm   fish   faith
shoal   freedom   flock   anger
grass   ball   hope   bike   herd

Concrete nouns: ....

Abstract nouns: ....

Collective nouns: ....

2 **Rewrite the sentences below replacing the underlined nouns with your own nouns.**

To get to the <u>school</u>, I pass a field with a <u>herd</u> of <u>cows</u>.

....

The <u>fear</u> I feel about going to <u>Aberdeen</u> on the <u>bus</u> is overwhelming.

....

Now Try This — Write a sentence that contains a concrete noun, an abstract noun and a collective noun.

Verbs

Verbs are doing or being words. → Bill eats spiders.

Verbs change depending on who is doing the action.

I read comics.   She reads comics.

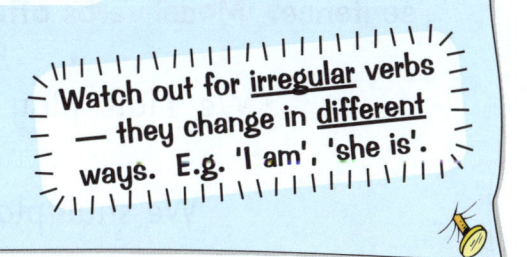

Watch out for irregular verbs — they change in different ways. E.g. 'I am', 'she is'.

1 Circle the correct form of each verb to finish these sentences.

Drew agrees / agree with his brother.

We is / are going to see / sees some friends tomorrow.

He always screams / scream when he sees a moth.

Ikenna often does / do his homework straight after school.

2 Rewrite each of these sentences so it is about you.

Arya is captain of the county football team.

....

Michelle usually dries her wet hair with a towel.

....

Raahim goes to night school twice a week.

....

Gregory has a new sports car.

....

Now Try This Can you use the verbs from question 1 to write your own sentences?

Section 1 — Word Types

Modal Verbs

Some verbs are used to give more information about the main verb in a sentence. Modal verbs often show how certain or possible something is.

We might play golf.   We will play golf.

We shall play golg.   We may play golf.

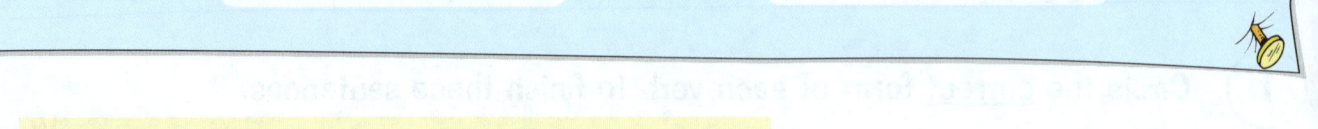

1) Circle the modal verbs in the sentences below.

I wouldn't want to be famous.

Yufei should know better.

Aiden should change his socks.

We shall do our very best.

Sitara may know the answer.

I could drive us there.

Sally might move to Canada.

She will give us some advice.

They can come too.

2) Circle the correct modal verbs to complete the sentences below.

Our holiday must / should have been relaxing, but it was very stressful.

I could / will have gone with Finlay, but I had other things to do.

That might / shall be the answer, but I'm not so sure.

Ken and Peter are away next week — they would / must let Chika know.

The builders knew they could / shall finish the job on time.

I'm really not sure about what to do — I might / would ask a friend.

Priti's not feeling well — she would / should stay in bed.

3 **Add the correct modal verb from the box to the sentences below.**

> could   might   would   should

I .... as well go to the party on my own.

Norman would go on holiday to Australia if he .... afford it.

.... you like a piece of apple crumble?

If you change your mind, you .... let me know.

4 **Write a sentence of your own using each of the modal verbs below.**

might

....

must

....

will

....

should

....

shall

....

Now Try This
"I might invent a time machine and visit the Vikings."
Make this sentence more certain by changing the modal verb.

Section 1 — Word Types

Adjectives

Adjectives are words that tell us **more** about a **noun**.

the soft pillow a tasty fish a lost dog the muddy field

1 Underline the adjectives in the phrases below.

Melissa's aggressive dog

a rare species

odd socks

purple spots

trendy music

cheeky children

a dismal day

crazy hair

unusual ideas

2 Replace the underlined adjectives with more interesting adjectives.

The play was good and the actors were good. I had a good time.

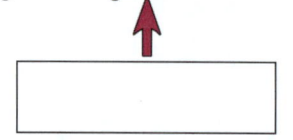

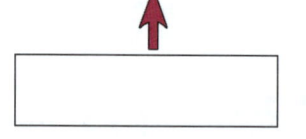

The concert was bad — the music was bad and the food was bad.

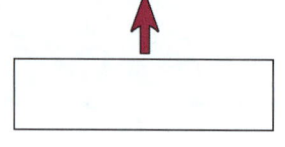

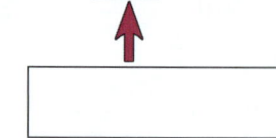

3 Add your own adjectives to the sentences below.

There was a .... noise coming from the kitchen.

The .... monster in the cave is very angry.

The .... monkeys will break our windscreen wipers.

Now Try This How many adjectives can you think of in one minute?

Section 1 — Word Types

Adverbs

Adverbs are words that describe verbs, adjectives and other adverbs.

I quickly ate my lunch.

'quickly' is the adverb.

The pudding was really tasty.

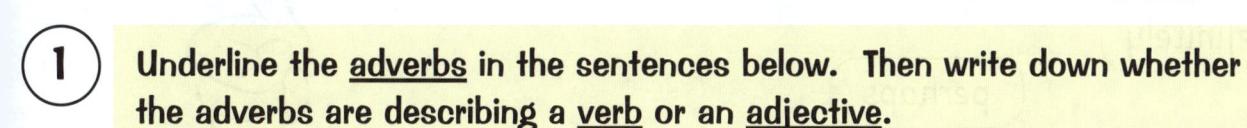

He didn't do very well.

1) Underline the adverbs in the sentences below. Then write down whether the adverbs are describing a verb or an adjective.

She played well. ➡ ....

The party was bitterly disappointing. ➡ ....

The car is incredibly dirty. ➡ ....

Louise cheerfully waved to us. ➡ ....

Sam seems extremely pleased. ➡ ....

2) Add the correct adverb from the box to the sentences below.

| very | elegantly | severely | truthfully | accidentally |

Tamina .... broke her mum's favourite vase.

Olivia said she didn't feel .... well.

That house is .... damaged.

The swans swam .... across the lake.

The schoolboy .... answered the teacher's questions.

Section 1 — Word Types

Some adverbs show how possible something is.

Surely they'll have a buffet.

Perhaps they'll have a buffet.

> Modal verbs also show how possible something is — take a look back at page 6.

3 Draw lines from the adverbs below to the correct label.

- definitely
- perhaps
- maybe
- possibly
- surely
- certainly

certain

not certain

4 Rewrite the sentences below, replacing the underlined adverbs with a less certain adverb. Use a different adverb for each sentence.

It's definitely true that the weather wasn't good enough.

....

Setting a deadline will certainly make a difference.

....

My car will probably break down on the way.

....

Section 1 — Word Types

5 Rewrite the sentences below, replacing the underlined adverbs with a more certain adverb. Use a different adverb for each sentence.

We will probably go to see Grandma tomorrow.

....

Francis and Gillian are possibly going to the cinema tonight.

....

Maybe Ulvertown Rovers will win the league.

....

6 Write each of the adverbs below in a sentence.

perhaps

....

surely

....

maybe

....

definitely

....

Now Try This — Think of three things you would like to do when you are older. Use adverbs to describe how likely you think each one is.

Section 1 — Word Types

Pronouns

Pronouns are words that you use to **replace nouns**.

> The boy found the ball, and he kicked it.

The pronouns help you avoid repeating 'the boy' and 'the ball'.

They can make your writing **flow** better and make it easier to **understand**.

> That's Jen's brother. He's older than her.

'He' refers to Jen's brother and 'her' refers to Jen.

1 Rewrite each sentence, replacing the underlined nouns with pronouns.

Charlotte made a picture for Trudy, then gave <u>the picture</u> to <u>Trudy</u>.

....

Ed and Saira lost Zac, so <u>Ed and Saira</u> went to look for <u>Zac</u>.

....

2 Use the pronouns to finish the story. Use each pronoun once.

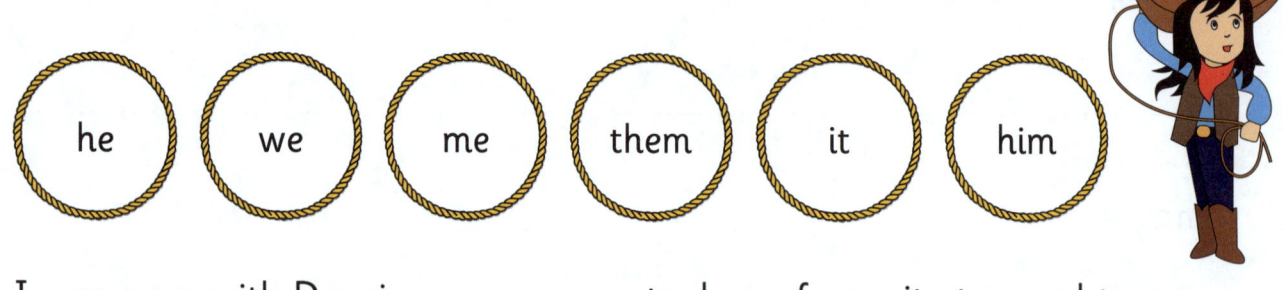

(he) (we) (me) (them) (it) (him)

I was cross with Dennis — .... took my favourite top and tore

.... He was sorry and said he would buy .... a new one.

My sister was angry with .... too — he borrowed her scissors and

broke .... But never mind, ... are all friends again now.

Now Try This

"Tegan and I started a jigsaw, and Tegan and I finished the jigsaw."
How could you use pronouns to make this sentence less repetitive?

Section 1 — Word Types

Relative Pronouns

Relative pronouns are words like 'who' and 'which'. They are used to join parts of sentences together.

See page 16 for more on relative pronouns.

I saw the girl who took Eli's drink. ← 'who' is used for people

Darrel only eats cakes which are sugar-free. ← 'which' is used for things

1) Draw lines to show which relative pronoun is missing from the sentences below.

We met the acrobat .... performed in the circus.

I like the blue shoes .... have sparkly laces.

They always stay in hotels .... have a five-star rating.

Joel is the builder .... built our house.

Lauren saw the dentist .... gave her a filling.

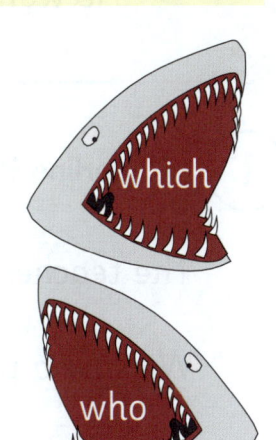

'which'

'who'

2) Add a relative pronoun from the box to the sentences below.

> that   whose   which   who

We have a new neighbour .... works at the bank.

This is the shop .... sells diving equipment.

Geraldine owns a house .... has four bedrooms.

That's the woman .... daughter is a famous footballer.

Now Try This — Write four new sentences using the relative pronouns from question 2.

Section 1 — Word Types

Determiners

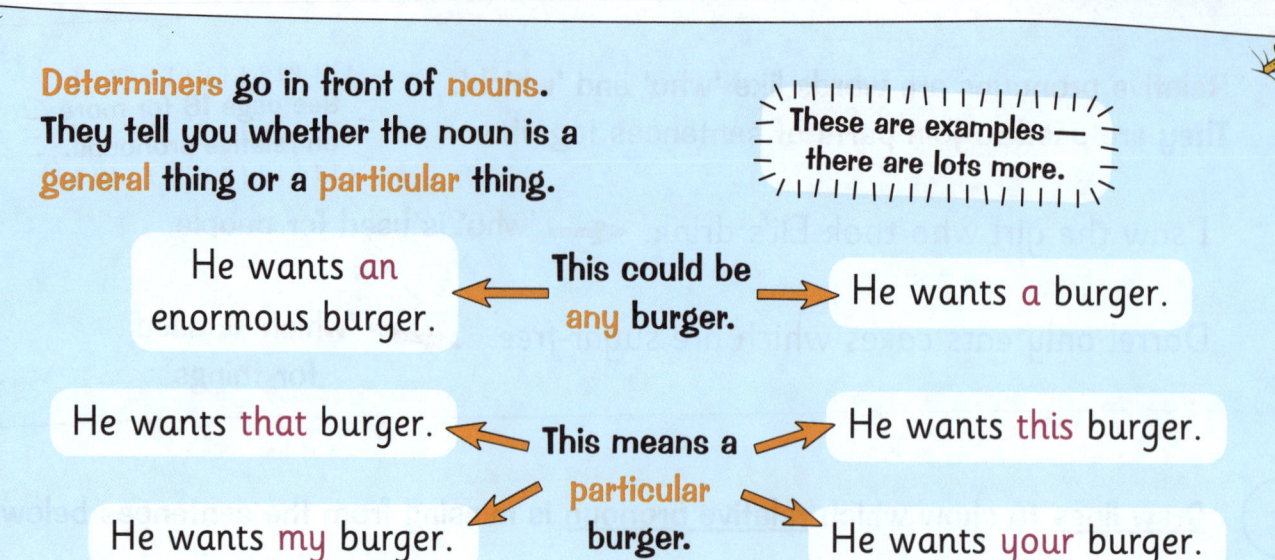

Determiners go in front of nouns. They tell you whether the noun is a general thing or a particular thing.

These are examples — there are lots more.

He wants an enormous burger. ← This could be any burger. → He wants a burger.

He wants that burger. ← This means a particular burger. → He wants this burger.

He wants my burger. ← → He wants your burger.

1) Underline the determiners in the sentences below.

The teacher told us a funny story about an elephant in the jungle.

We saw a picture of that house by the river where your boat is.

Ben and Euan finally changed those light bulbs in their bathroom.

A police officer chased some thieves out of the bank and into an alleyway.

2) Add a determiner correctly to the sentences so that they make sense.

Tip: there's more than one correct answer to some of these questions.

.... pizza is the best pizza I've ever tasted.

We need to go to the garage — .... car has broken down.

Add .... milk — any amount is fine.

Kelly saw .... aardvark and .... lion at the zoo.

Now Try This — Have another look at question 2. How many different determiners can you use to complete the sentences so that they still make sense?

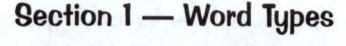

Section 1 — Word Types

Section 2 — Clauses and Phrases

Clauses

Most sentences are made of clauses.
A main clause has a subject and a verb, and makes sense on its own.
A subordinate clause gives extra information but it doesn't make sense on its own.

main clause ➡ Hilary told Libby that she couldn't come. ⬅ subordinate clause

1) Tick the sentences where the main clause is underlined.

<u>Darius went to the shop</u> because he needed some milk. ☐

Jodie is going to the party <u>even if Rebecca won't go with her</u>. ☐

<u>Provided that it doesn't start to rain</u>, they'll play outside. ☐

Unless you know the answer, <u>we'll ask Zeynep</u>. ☐

<u>They climbed the tree</u> even though I thought it was a bad idea. ☐

2) Add a word from the box and your own clause to complete the sentences below.

| when | after | although | until | before |

Only use each word from the box once.

We need to wait ………………………………………………………

Eleanor has a shower ………………………………………………

I'm going to buy some sweets ……………………………………

Doris wants to get a dog …………………………………………

Abeba eats her breakfast …………………………………………

Now Try This: Write three sentences about your weekend that include subordinate clauses.

Basic Relative Clauses

A **relative clause** is a **subordinate clause** that is often introduced by a **relative pronoun**. Here are some relative pronouns: **that**, **which**, **whose** and **who**. The words **where** and **when** can also introduce relative clauses.

Joe is the man <u>who delivers the milk</u>.
relative pronoun → ← relative clause

1 Circle the <u>relative pronouns</u> in the sentences below. Then underline the <u>relative clause</u> in each sentence.

I prefer the blue shoes which match my dress.

This is the house that Megan is going to move into.

I don't like people who are cruel to animals.

We found a lost dog whose owner was nowhere to be seen.

Yvonne likes to go for walks that have amazing views.

This is the computer game that I bought last weekend.

2 Add a suitable <u>relative pronoun</u> to complete the <u>relative clauses</u> below.

This is the book ………… Pria was reading.

The Tasty Taverna is a restaurant ………… specialises in vegetarian meals.

I need to find a shop ………… sells fancy dress costumes.

Ulrika met a man ………… dog was almost as big as he was.

Juliet is the person ………… always gets her own way.

Let's go on holiday to a country ………… has hot, sunny weather.

We saw a jellyfish ………… tentacles were two metres long.

3 Draw lines from each main clause to the correct relative clause to make a sentence.

Main Clause	Relative Clause
I found an injured rabbit	who can renovate our house.
Scott moved to a quiet village	when he got lost at the funfair.
Mum is looking for a builder	that he saw advertised on TV.
Themba remembers the day	whose leg was broken.
Colin wants to buy the game	where there were no other children.

4 Add a relative clause using 'who' or 'which' to each sentence below.

Susanna waited for Edward ....

There was a lot of noise ....

Ronald went to the circus ....

The people welcomed the man ....

5 Write two sentences which contain a relative clause using the words below.

(teacher   busy)

....

(scientist   experiment)

....

Now Try This Find a page in a newspaper, book or magazine and see how many relative clauses you can spot. Can you underline the relative pronoun in each one?

Section 2 — Clauses and Phrases

Trickier Relative Clauses

A relative clause sometimes comes in the middle of a sentence.

The girl <u>who</u> knocked on the door ran away.

relative pronoun   relative clause

The ball <u>which</u> flew past us landed in the garden.

relative pronoun   relative clause

1 Underline the relative clause in each of the sentences below.

Hibo, who wants to be a pilot, is taking flying lessons.

After the party, which finished at midnight, we went to bed.

The room where the books are stored is being repainted.

That day when I fell over was the most embarrassing day of my life.

The house that flooded during the storm can now be lived in again.

Eugeniusz, whose son plays the drums in a band, loves rock music.

2 Add a suitable relative clause to complete the sentences below.

The boy .... looked very angry.

Michael's phone .... broke.

The town .... is not very big.

Roger's nephew .... is twelve.

That windy day .... was awful.

My old teddy bear .... is in the wash.

Section 2 — Clauses and Phrases

Relative clauses don't always have a relative pronoun —
sometimes the relative pronoun can be left out.

They got the postcard which we sent from Spain.
relative clause with a relative pronoun

They got the postcard we sent from Spain.
relative clause without a relative pronoun

3 Tick the sentences that can also be written without a relative pronoun.

The relative clauses are underlined.

I know a girl who says she's Lisa's friend. ☐

The museum which we visited was very interesting. ☐

Nobody knows the boy whose parents are abroad. ☐

That's the football team that Josh is joining. ☐

My tenth birthday was the day that I was chased by a squirrel. ☐

4 Rewrite the sentences below without a relative pronoun.

The walk which we went on was far too long.

....

I've forgotten the name of the film which Jim recommended.

....

She can't remember the day that we went to the zoo.

....

Now Try This — Write two sentences about your day that contain a relative clause but don't need a relative pronoun.

Phrases

Clauses and sentences are built up of groups of words called phrases. A phrase either doesn't have a verb, or doesn't have a subject (some phrases might have neither).

to the post office   a few green monsters

1) Draw lines to match each group of words with the correct label.

	Phrase	
behind the blue sofa		we're happy
on the phone		those naughty boys
he's silly		let's play golf
little pork sausages		I go swimming
Ray sat down	Clause	they're fine
at the back		long, hairy legs

2) Underline the longest noun phrase in each sentence.

Riku lost his red, fluffy mittens.

The man in the waterproof coat ate a sandwich.

One type of penguin lives in South Africa.

Willow read a long book about a yam called Gavin.

The big dog ran after the bouncing yellow tennis ball.

A tired explorer with a big backpack walked over the high mountain range.

A noun phrase is a group of words that contains a noun and any words that describe it.

Now Try This — What is the longest noun phrase you can think of? Use it in a sentence.

Section 2 — Clauses and Phrases

Section 3 — Conjunctions and Prepositions

Co-ordinating Conjunctions

Co-ordinating conjunctions are words that join two main clauses together. You can remember them using FANBOYS: For And Nor But Or Yet So

We bought some flour <u>and</u> we bought some cheese.

main clause — co-ordinating conjunction — main clause

1) Add the co-ordinating conjunctions from the box to the sentences below.

> for   but   so   or   and

Use each word in the box once.

I'd like to go to Australia, ... it's too expensive.

In the cellar it was dark, ... there were lots of strange noises.

Please give this letter to a parent, ... give it to a guardian.

Playing near busy roads is dangerous, ... you shouldn't do it.

Mabel felt completely relaxed, ... she was on holiday.

2) Join each pair of sentences using 'but', 'and' or 'so'.

I would like a drink. I would like some food.

....

Fran's remark was hurtful. It was also true.

....

My pencil was blunt. I used a pen.

....

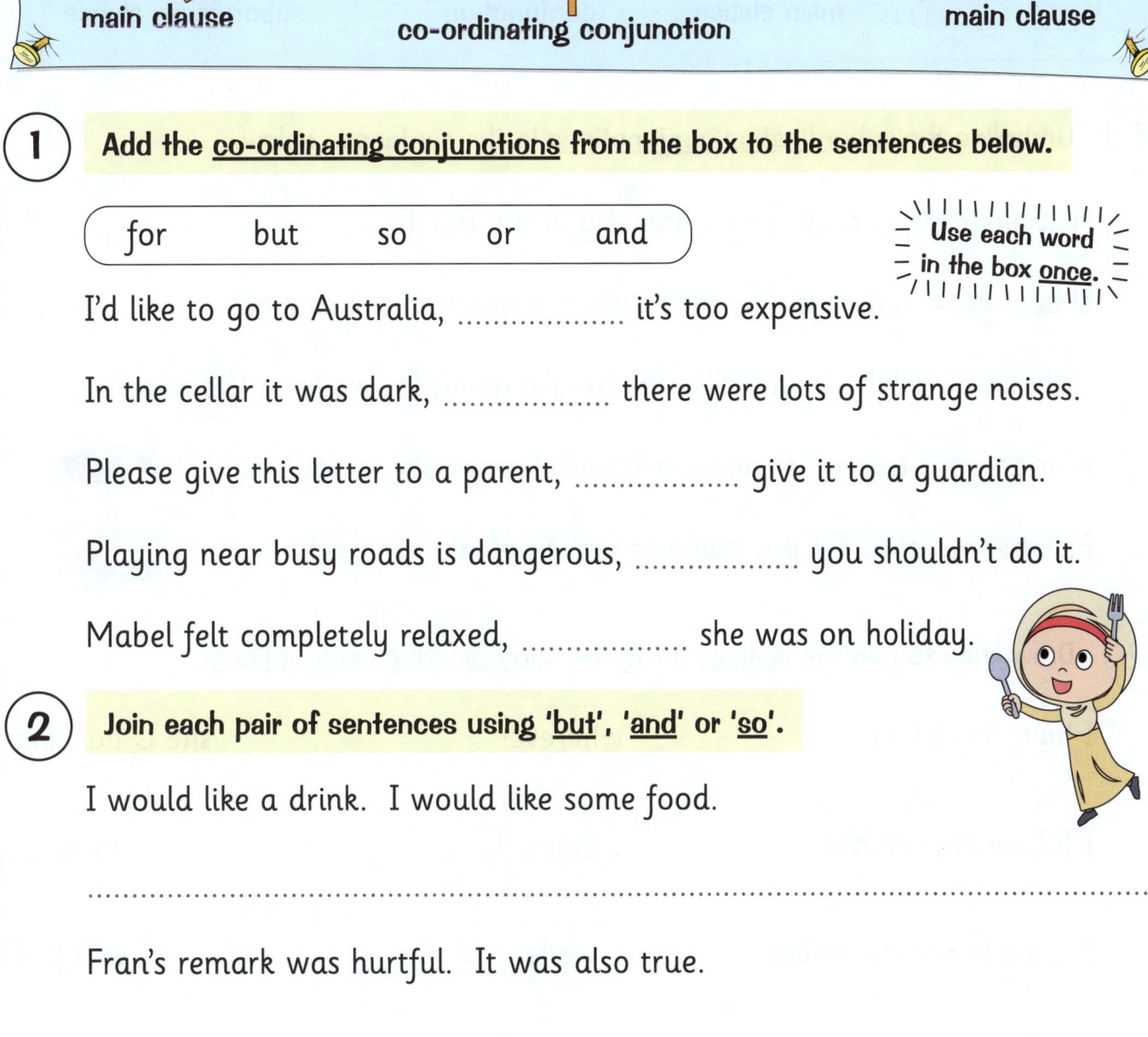

Now Try This — Try writing a sentence that includes 'nor' and another that uses 'yet'.

Subordinating Conjunctions

Subordinating conjunctions are words that link a **main clause** to a **subordinate clause**. These conjunctions can go at the **start** of a sentence, or in the **middle**.

See p. 15 for more about clauses.

I am staying here <u>until</u> Gran comes.

main clause   conjunction   subordinate clause

1) Underline the subordinating conjunctions in the sentences below.

Help yourself to a glass of water if you are thirsty.

Unless your dad says you can't, you can come to the cinema.

Although it might sound silly, I quite like going for walks in the rain.

Marian goes to see her uncle in hospital when she is not busy.

Fletcher watches TV programmes while he eats his lunch.

2) Draw lines to join the clauses using the subordinating conjunctions.

I have lived here	wherever	she is dancing.
I follow my brother	since	he goes.
My sister always smiles	while	I was five.
I like Pierre	because	he can be a bit annoying.
The dog can't come in	even though	his paws are dirty.

Now Try This — Write five sentences of your own using the subordinating conjunctions from question 2. Three of your sentences should start with the conjunction.

Section 3 — Conjunctions and Prepositions

Using Conjunctions for Cohesion

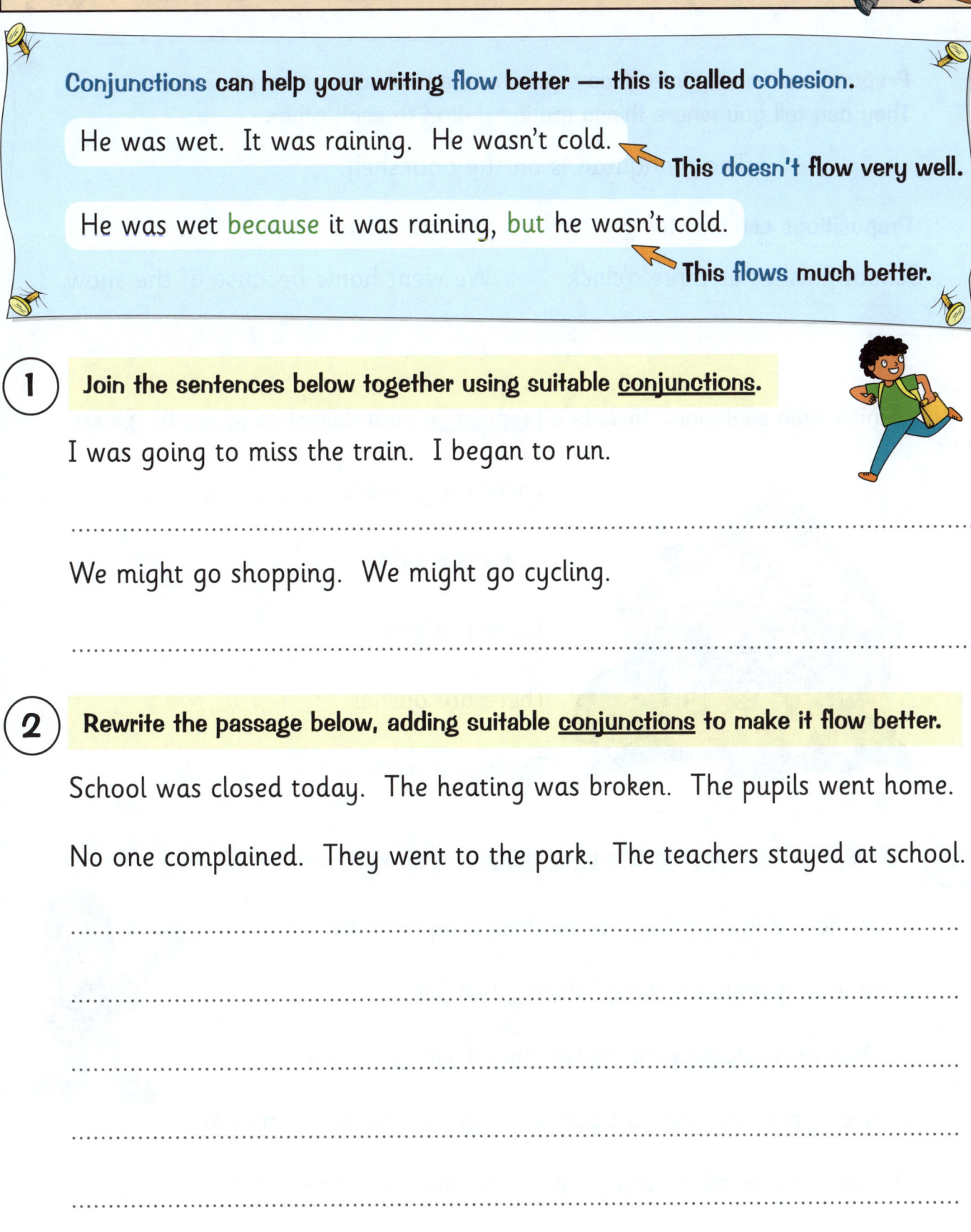

Conjunctions can help your writing flow better — this is called cohesion.

> He was wet. It was raining. He wasn't cold.

This doesn't flow very well.

> He was wet because it was raining, but he wasn't cold.

This flows much better.

1) Join the sentences below together using suitable <u>conjunctions</u>.

I was going to miss the train. I began to run.

....

We might go shopping. We might go cycling.

....

2) Rewrite the passage below, adding suitable <u>conjunctions</u> to make it flow better.

School was closed today. The heating was broken. The pupils went home.

No one complained. They went to the park. The teachers stayed at school.

....

....

....

....

....

Now Try This — Think of four short sentences to continue the passage in question 2. Use conjunctions to link your sentences and make them flow.

Section 3 — Conjunctions and Prepositions

Prepositions

Prepositions usually introduce a pronoun, a noun or a noun phrase.
They can tell you where things are in relation to each other.

> The orangutan is on the bookshelf.

Prepositions can also tell you when or why something happens.

> School finishes at three o'clock. We went home because of the snow.

1 Finish each sentence. Include a preposition so it describes where things are.

There are flowers ....

There is a bird ....

There is a tree ....

There are bushes ....

There is a path ....

2 Circle the most appropriate preposition in the sentences below.

That picture in / on the wall is absolutely horrible.

I ate lots of popcorn since / during the film.

Iris has been playing the guitar since / while 10 pm.

Jamila is meeting her dad above / in front of the supermarket.

We can't do anything until / while the day after tomorrow.

Let's put up posters in / before any available space.

They buried the time capsule underneath / over the oak tree.

3 Choose a suitable preposition from the box to complete each sentence.

| after | from | during | on | outside | until | in |

.... Friday, I'm going to the dentist.

I think there's a mistake .... my work.

The woman in the cinema told us to stop talking .... the film.

Our school is open .... 8 am .... 4 pm.

The shop isn't open, so people are forming a queue .... the door.

I always listen to music .... dinner.

4 Write a sentence including at least two prepositions.

....

....

5 Describe your bedroom using prepositions correctly.

....

....

....

....

Now Try This: Choose three things that you can see right now.
Use prepositions to describe where they are in relation to one another.

Section 4 — Linking Ideas

Linking Ideas in a Paragraph

Adverbial phrases tell you how, when, where or how often something happens. They help your writing flow smoothly, which is called cohesion.

In ten minutes, we're going to the park. We're having lunch after that.

The adverbial phrases help these two sentences to flow together by telling you how the two events are linked.

1) Circle all the adverbial phrases in the box below.

> over there   twice a year   my cat   near the wall
> after a while   winter weather   this ketchup
> his horse   every time   the other day   very slowly

2) Underline the adverbial phrase in each pair of sentences.

I can play the flute. <u>Last year</u>, I learnt to play the recorder.

The chest was unlocked. Without a sound, Susie opened the lid.

It's a hot day. You should put suncream on after lunch.

I do after-school activities four times a week. It's exhausting but fun.

There are one hundred tadpoles in the school pond. We're studying them.

The bus arrived. Thomas ate his breakfast ridiculously fast.

There was so much to do. Tina didn't stop painting until midnight.

My bedroom was a mess. I hid all the toys and books under the bed.

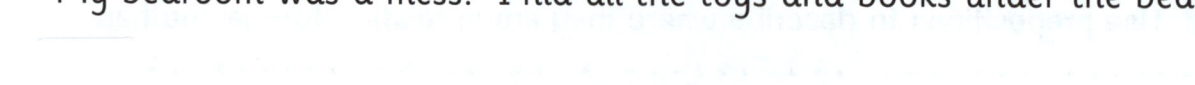

3 Use the timetable for an activity day to put the missing words below into the paragraph.

~~Yesterday~~   in the garden   At 10 am

in two separate teams   after lunch

Finally   First

9 am	10 am	Midday	1 pm	3 pm
Registration and warm-up games	Obstacle course races	Lunch in the garden	Building a tree house	Making rafts and racing them in groups

...Yesterday..., I went to an amazing activity day. .... we had to register, and then we played some warm-up games. ...., we raced each other through a great obstacle course. We ate ...., and .... we built a big tree house. .... we made rafts and raced them ....

4 Rewrite each pair of sentences, adding the adverbial phrase in the box.

If an adverbial phrase is at the start of a sentence, you put a comma after it.

I love football. I go to training. [on Mondays]
I love football. On Mondays, I go to training.

I am making a kite. I will try it out. [after tea]

....

The witch looked around. She crept up the stairs. [very quietly]

....

It is Christmas Eve. It will be Christmas Day. [tomorrow morning]

....

Now Try This: Describe your morning routine, using adverbial phrases to link your sentences.

Section 4 — Linking Ideas

Linking Paragraphs

You can use adverbs and other adverbial phrases to link paragraphs together smoothly.

It was four o'clock, and old Mr Coxton was sleeping soundly in his chair. Nearby, Mrs Smith was weeding her garden. She sang as she went along.

Choosing the right tense will also help to link your paragraphs together.

1 Read each of these paragraph beginnings. Draw a line to show whether the underlined word or phrase shows a change in time, place or number.

Later, the nurse looked at my ankle. She said it was broken in two places.

Thirdly, I started to screw the different pieces together, one at a time.

At Grandad's house, Clare set up the chessboard and made two cups of tea.

time

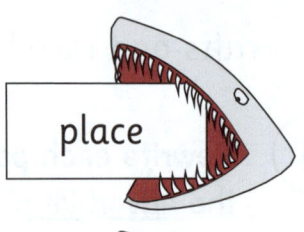

place

number

2 Draw lines to show whether each word or phrase would link paragraphs by time, place or number.

in Ian's room   before breakfast   at the garage

this week   PLACE   fourthly

secondly   NUMBER   above that

next to him   behind me

TIME   every day

thirdly   at 5 pm   firstly

Section 4 — Linking Ideas

3 Use one of the words or phrases from the middle row to link these paragraphs.

In the morning, George went to buy the ingredients for his lemon cake. It took over an hour.

................................, he started mixing and measuring.

Secondly, I covered the exercise book in colourful patterned paper.

................................, I used some sticky plastic to make the book waterproof and keep it looking neat.

(That afternoon) (Under the table) (Last week) (Thirdly)

My brother Jeremy loves doing science experiments — even in the house!

................................, he mixed lots of Mum's hair products together. It exploded everywhere!

I was really enjoying the spaghetti Dad had made for tea, but I kept dropping bits accidentally.

................................, our cat was eating the scraps, but he couldn't manage the spaghetti!

4 Complete the second paragraph below by putting the verbs in brackets into the right tense.

I am sitting at the table, trying not to look at the fridge.

I know I shouldn't open it, but the temptation is just too strong.

I creep over and open the door, desperate to get a peek at my birthday cake.

My uncle always (**to bake**) .... me a special cake. Last year, he (**to come**) .... to my party with a giant sprout.

I (**to be**) .... horrified! But when he cut it open, it wasn't a sprout at all! He (**to make**) .... a chocolate cake that looked like a sprout. This year's cake (**to look**) .... even more extraordinary.

Now Try This Add two more paragraphs to the story in question 4. Use adverbial phrases and tense choices to link your paragraphs together smoothly.

Section 4 — Linking Ideas

Section 5 — Verb Tenses

Present Tense and Past Tense

Use the simple present tense to write about something that happens regularly.

Ellie cheats.   Hassan knits.   Tom forgets things.

Use the simple past tense to write about something that's finished.

Ellie cheated.   Hassan knitted.   Tom forgot things.

1 Underline the simple present tense verb in each sentence and then rewrite the sentence in the simple past tense.

Dan <u>borrows</u> a book. ➡ Dan borrowed a book.

We pack the car. ➡ ....

I pay the bills. ➡ ....

They throw it out. ➡ ....

He paints a picture. ➡ ....

Yaling does a lot. ➡ ....

2 Write a simple present tense sentence and a simple past tense sentence about each picture. Use a different verb in each sentence.

Present ....

Past ....

Present ....

Past ....

Now Try This: Rewrite your present tense sentences from question 2 in the simple past tense, and your past tense sentences in the simple present tense.

Verbs with 'ing'

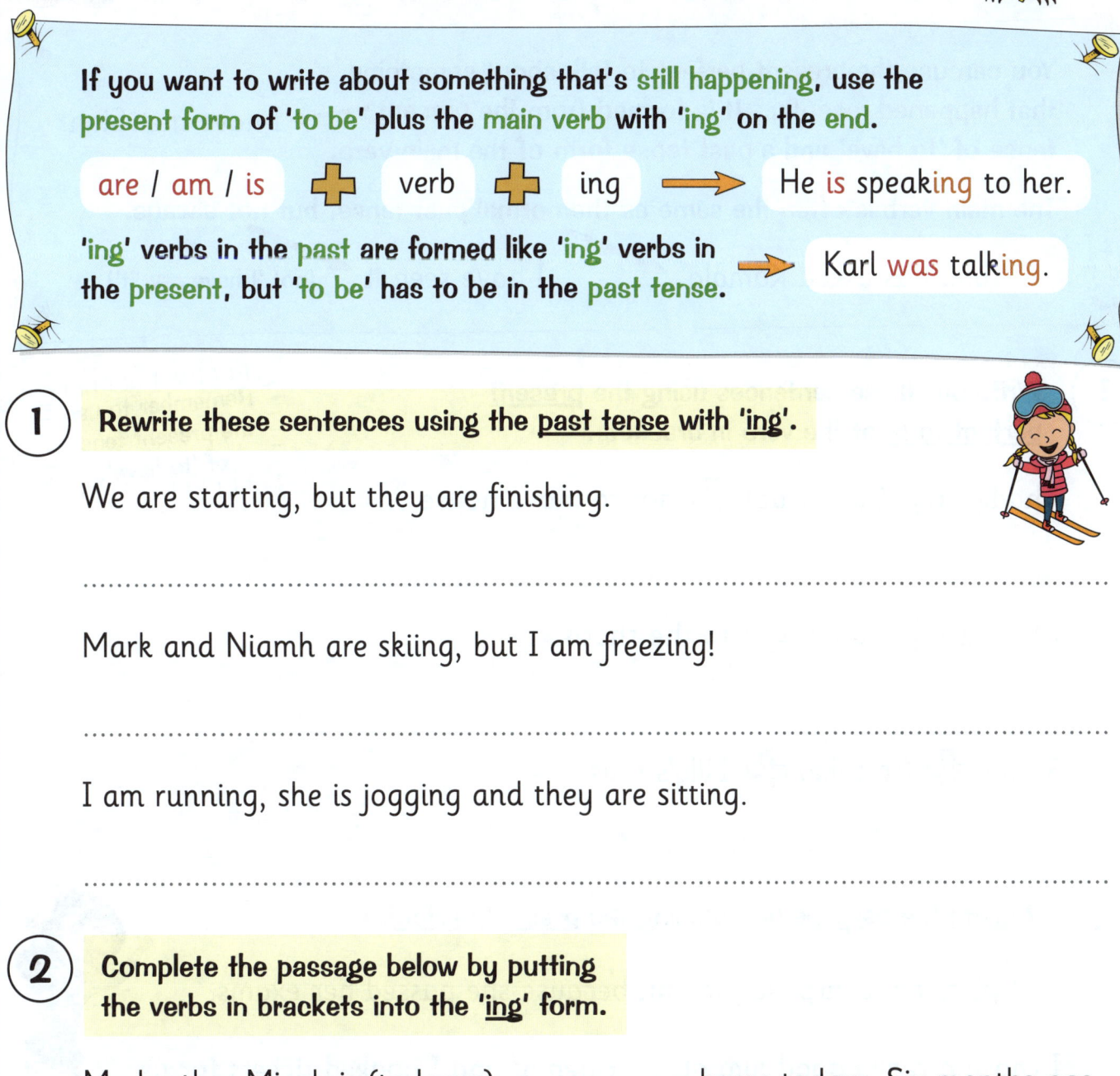

If you want to write about something that's still happening, use the present form of 'to be' plus the main verb with 'ing' on the end.

are / am / is ➕ verb ➕ ing ➡ He is speaking to her.

'ing' verbs in the past are formed like 'ing' verbs in the present, but 'to be' has to be in the past tense. ➡ Karl was talking.

1 Rewrite these sentences using the past tense with 'ing'.

We are starting, but they are finishing.

....

Mark and Niamh are skiing, but I am freezing!

....

I am running, she is jogging and they are sitting.

....

2 Complete the passage below by putting the verbs in brackets into the 'ing' form.

My brother Micah is (to leave) .... home today. Six months ago he was (to apply) .... to boarding school, and he was (to hope) .... to get a place. Now he's actually (to go) .... I will miss him because he's always (to help) .... me with my homework. I am already (to count) .... down the days until half term.

Now Try This Write a paragraph about what a friend is doing right now using 'ing' verbs.

Section 5 — Verb Tenses

The Present Perfect

You can use the **present perfect** to talk about something that **happened recently**. It is formed from the **present tense** of 'to have' and a **past tense form** of the **main verb**.

→ I **have met** Sian.

The main verb is **often** the same as the **normal past tense**, but not always.

Tony **has asked** Kamala.   I **have seen** it.   (not 'I have **saw** it')

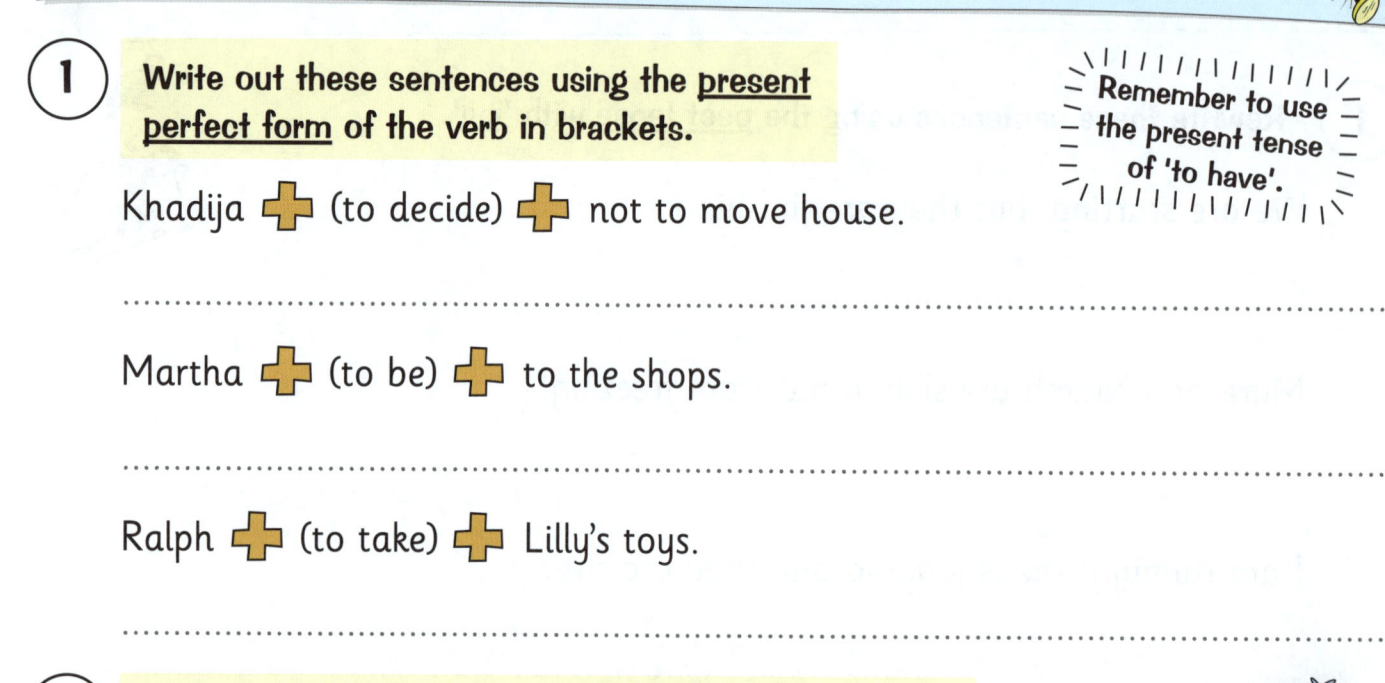

1) Write out these sentences using the **present perfect form** of the verb in brackets.

Remember to use the present tense of 'to have'.

Khadija ✚ (to decide) ✚ not to move house.

....

Martha ✚ (to be) ✚ to the shops.

....

Ralph ✚ (to take) ✚ Lilly's toys.

....

2) Rewrite the passage below using the present perfect.

   I planned a surprise for Ann because she passed her exams.
I chose a really good film at the cinema, and I booked tickets for us.

....

....

....

....

Now Try This — The verb 'to see' has a different form in the simple past tense and in the present perfect. How many other verbs can you think of that are like this?

Section 5 — Verb Tenses

Section 6 — Standard and Non-Standard English

Standard and Non-Standard English

Standard English is the formal type of writing that you should use in your written work. It helps make your writing clearer.

Standard English → We are the best team.   I haven't seen him.

non-Standard English → We is the best team.   I ain't seen him.

1 Write 'S' next to the sentences written in Standard English and 'N' next to the ones written in non-Standard English.

She were an amazing player. ☐   I will played sport later. ☐

I am going fishing today. ☐   That are an awful story. ☐

Last week, I run five miles. ☐   We are listening to music. ☐

Have you finished your dinner? ☐   I eat two muffins yesterday. ☐

You are very tall, Mr Grew. ☐   I am building a spaceship. ☐

2 Cross out the incorrect options in brackets so that these sentences are in Standard English.

Kevin must (have / of) (gone / went) on another special mission.

I would (have / of) asked Stuart, but he (gone / went) home.

You should (have / of) asked before you (done / did) it without me.

I (saw / seen) my grandparents earlier when they (came / come) over.

Abdul (come / came) downstairs because he had (done / did) his homework.

We might (have / of) left the pencils where we (done / did) the drawing.

3. Write the correct word to complete each sentence in Standard English.

them / those

Go and ask .... people if they'll help us carry it.

I was so hungry that I ate .... all in one go.

Take .... photos over to the windowsill, please.

I saw .... steal the stickers at lunchtime.

me / I

Nicola and .... both play the trombone.

My cousin is teaching .... to do karate.

It's my turn because they found .... first.

Oli and .... are planning a surprise party.

'I' is a subject and 'me' is an object.

4. Circle the verbs that are not in the correct form and write the correct form of the verb below. The first one has been done for you.

My parents (has) just bought a bakery. It are just down the road from our

have ....

house. I is helping them to get it ready for the grand opening. Dad say

....

the decorating is finished so now we is getting the food ready. Mum and

....

Dad are great bakers. Dad bake all the bread and cakes, and Mum do

....

everything else. I hope lots of people visits the bakery when it opens.

....

In **Standard English**, only use **one negative** word to make the meaning negative. → I don't know.

Double negatives are **non-Standard English**. → I don't know nothing.

'Ain't' is **non-Standard English**. → We ain't coming.

5 Write '2' next to the double negative sentences and '1' next to those with one negative.

I haven't got nothing. ☐   David doesn't like broccoli. ☐

My dad hasn't got a beard. ☐   You can't see nothing in here. ☐

We don't have no biscuits left. ☐   No one said nothing to me. ☐

Connor won't go nowhere. ☐   We mustn't do anything yet. ☐

I can't tell you the secret. ☐   Oliver couldn't find anyone. ☐

They haven't got a sister. ☐   Ha-Yun wasn't helping no one. ☐

6 Rewrite these sentences in Standard English.

I ain't very well. → ....

We ain't sure. → ....

Raj ain't going. → ....

Chloe ain't got it. → ....

I ain't finished. → ....

He ain't here. → ....

Now Try This Rewrite the sentences from question 5 that contain double negatives so that they are in Standard English.

Section 7 — Sentence Punctuation

Capital Letters and Full Stops

Sentences always start with a capital letter and often finish with a full stop. Sentences with a full stop are often statements (sentences that tell you something). Use capital letters for I and for names of people, places or things.

On Wednesday, I am going to London with my sister.

1 Circle the words below that should have capital letters.

| eiffel tower | castle | tomorrow | spain |
| ashley | city | friday | christmas |

2 Put a tick next to the sentences that use capital letters and full stops correctly and put a cross next to the ones that don't.

mrs Flint is thirty-two her birthday is in may. ☐

My step-mum's favourite sweets can only be bought in Canada. ☐

My Best Friend is called Amy. She lives in Bath ☐

Ellis's dog is called Spot. Spot is a Dalmatian. ☐

I play cricket every Friday evening. ☐

Rewrite the incorrect sentences with capital letters and full stops in the right places.

....

....

Now Try This Write a sentence that uses 'I', a sentence that uses a name and a sentence that uses a month. Make sure you use capital letters correctly.

Question Marks

Questions always end with a **question mark** and often begin with a **question word**.

When are we leaving?   Why are you running?

1 Draw lines to match each sentence to the correct punctuation mark.

Where are you going on holiday   Are you feeling OK, Kinga

Here are those gloves you lost   I don't know how to fry an egg

Let's go shopping tomorrow   What's happening out there

Is this your idea of a joke   It's raining a lot this week

Would you like ketchup   We should order pizzas

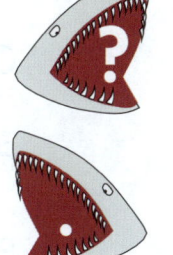

2 Write a question to match each of the answers given below.

Q: ....

A: I will. I'm excellent at map-reading.

Q: ....

A: A packed lunch and a waterproof jacket.

Use a capital letter to start your sentence, and a question mark at the end.

Q: ....

A: No thanks, I'm a vegetarian.

Q: ....

A: Yes, that's fine. I'll come at six o'clock.

Now Try This — Imagine you are interviewing your favourite celebrity. Write down the first three questions you would ask them.

Section 7 — Sentence Punctuation

Exclamation Marks

Exclamation marks show that something is said **loudly** or with **strong emotion**. → That's amazing!

Exclamation marks are also used for strong commands. → Go away!

But if the command **isn't urgent** or strong, use a **full stop**. → Pass the salt.

1) Tick the three <u>commands</u> which are most likely to end with an <u>exclamation mark</u>.

Shut up ☐   Quick, get out of here ☐

Let me help you ☐   Please wait here ☐

Stop that, now ☐   Please stop crying ☐

2) Use <u>full stops</u> and <u>exclamation marks</u> to complete these sentences.

Ouch, that really hurt .....

My brother is really good at playing the piano .....

Watch out, it's going to fall over .....

The bathroom is the second door on the left .....

3) Write two sentences using some words from the box and an <u>exclamation mark</u>.

| wonderful   terrible   day   party |

....

....

Now Try This — Write a sentence ending with an exclamation mark that you might say if someone gave you an exciting gift.

Section 7 — Sentence Punctuation

Sentence Practice

Remember — sentences should always start with a **capital letter**.
They can end with a **full stop**, a **question mark** or an **exclamation mark**.

1 Write the most likely <u>final punctuation</u> at the end of each sentence. Then write whether each sentence is a <u>question</u>, an <u>exclamation</u>, a <u>command</u> or a <u>statement</u>.

John asked when they were leaving... ➡ ....

How ridiculous those shoes are... ➡ ....

Switch the appliance off at the mains... ➡ ....

What time do you think we should leave... ➡ ....

What an incredible cake that is... ➡ ....

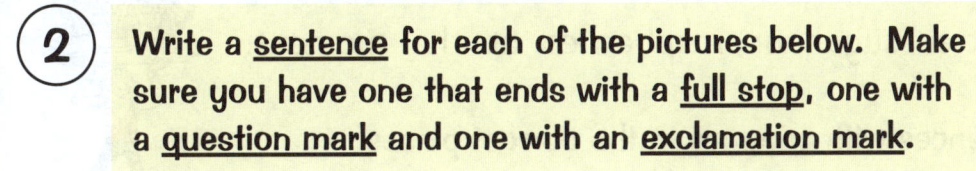

2 Write a <u>sentence</u> for each of the pictures below. Make sure you have one that ends with a <u>full stop</u>, one with a <u>question mark</u> and one with an <u>exclamation mark</u>.

Now Try This Write three commands that your teacher might give to your class. Remember to use the correct punctuation.

Section 7 — Sentence Punctuation

Section 8 — Commas

Commas in Lists

Use **commas** to separate *items in a list*. There should be a comma between each thing in a list except the last two. These two are separated with 'and' or 'or'.

> I donated three films, two books, some old clothes and a really difficult puzzle.

1) Add commas in the correct places in this paragraph.

I am going to the supermarket with my mum her sister and my best friend. We need to buy some more cereal a couple of pints of milk a pack of dishcloths and some baking ingredients. We are going to bake some chocolate-chip cookies a batch of flapjacks a sponge cake and a raspberry cheesecake. We haven't got any flour butter sugar or raspberries at the moment.

2) Rewrite these sentences with commas in the correct places.

You will need 500 g sugar 200 g flour 300 g butter and some raisins.

....
....

Please bring a packed lunch a swimming costume and a few pens.

....
....

The journey was quite long very tiring and really boring.

....
....

3 Write the items in the list into a __sentence__ using __commas__ in the correct places.

I need to ....

....

....

....

....

To do

clean the kitchen

bake some flapjacks

do my homework

tidy my bedroom

4 Use the items below to __complete the sentences__. Each list should have __four__ things in it. Remember to put __commas__ in the correct places.

a microwave   a brand-new camera   a herd of cows   lots of benches

a squirrel   a week's supply of cake   two theatre tickets   two rabbits

Enter the competition to win ....

....

....

On the walk we saw ....

....

....

Now Try This Write a sentence that lists at least three things you would take on a trip to the beach. Make sure you put commas in the right places.

Section 8 — Commas

Commas to Avoid Confusion

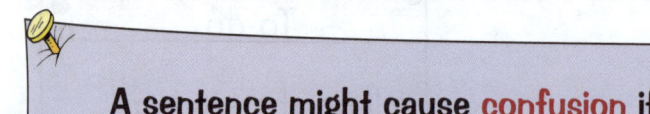

A sentence might cause confusion if there is more than one possible meaning. Commas help to avoid confusion by making it clearer what a sentence means.

Without commas, this sentence is confusing. → I invited my brothers Sam and Luke.

I invited my brothers, Sam and Luke.

I invited my brothers, Sam, and Luke.

Adding a comma (or two commas) makes the meaning of the sentence clearer.

The sentence with one comma suggests I invited my brothers, who are called Sam and Luke. The sentence with two commas suggests I invited my brothers as well as Sam and Luke.

It's OK to put a comma with 'and' if the sentence is confusing without one.

1 Add a <u>comma</u> to each sentence below to <u>change the meaning</u>.

No babies are cute.

I don't want to fight Jade.

Clara loves painting books and baking cakes.

I only told my parents, James and Aneesah.

2 Read the sentences below. Explain how the <u>meaning</u> of the sentence <u>changes</u> when the <u>comma</u> is added.

I am frightened of cricket bats and thunderstorms.

I am frightened of cricket, bats and thunderstorms.

....

....

....

3 Draw a picture in the box below each sentence to show what it means.

> The table was piled high with chocolate cake and crisps.

> The table was piled high with chocolate, cake and crisps.

4 Add a comma or commas to each sentence, so that it has the same meaning as the sentence in the box.

As the man turned blue doctors started to worry. → Doctors started to worry as the man turned blue.

Ella's favourite things are summer holidays and going on long walks. → Ella has three favourite things.

It's time to start cooking children. → I'm telling some children it's time to start cooking.

I took a photo of the woman with a camera. → I used a camera to take a photo of the woman.

Max the neighbour's cat is making strange noises. → A cat called Max is making strange noises.

Now Try This "Most of the time travellers choose to fly." Change the meaning of this sentence by adding a comma. Explain how the meaning has changed.

Section 8 — Commas

Commas After Subordinate Clauses

Use a comma to separate a main clause from a subordinate clause in a sentence — but only when the subordinate clause comes first.

While I'm at the gym, I listen to my music.

The main clause makes sense on its own. It's the most important part of a sentence.

You don't need a comma if the subordinate clause is at the end of a sentence.

I listen to my music while I'm at the gym.

A subordinate clause doesn't make sense on its own. It's less important than the main clause.

1) Add commas in the correct places in the sentences below.

As I ☐ got on the bus ☐ I ☐ dropped my bag.

Although ☐ I am scared ☐ of sharks ☐ I love visiting the aquarium.

Once ☐ I'd finished eating ☐ I started reading my new book.

Rather than ☐ going out ☐ we stayed in ☐ and watched a film.

2) Underline the subordinate clauses and add commas where needed.

While you were distracted I swapped our plates.

You can go to the party as long as you wear something sensible.

Now that you've told me that everything makes much more sense.

Until we've found the solution we'll keep trying to work it out.

I'll come and help you as soon as I can.

Since we're all here I'd like to tell you something.

Section 8 — Commas

3) Put commas in the sentences that need them.

I'm really tired because I've been walking all day.

When I realised what I'd done, I apologised immediately.

Bob started laughing after we'd told him the joke.

Although I like the album, this song isn't my favourite.

As you're older than me, you should go first.

4) Rewrite these sentences with commas in the correct places.

Even though it was cold I wanted ice cream.

....

Despite the fact we lost we still had fun.

....

Whereas Steffen is calm Nima is always stressed.

....

Before I left the house I turned the lights off.

....

5) Add a subordinate clause to complete each of these sentences. Remember to use commas correctly.

.... I need to ring my sister.

.... Raf wasn't offended.

.... Karthik wasn't scared.

Now Try This: Write three sentences about what you did last weekend. Each sentence should begin with a subordinate clause. Remember to use commas correctly.

Commas After Fronted Adverbials

A fronted adverbial is an adverbial phrase at the beginning of a sentence. Fronted adverbials tell you where, when, how or how often something happens. You need a comma after a fronted adverbial.

On my birthday, we went out for lunch.

1 Add commas in the correct places in the sentences below.

As quietly as possible Adil crept downstairs.

Very quickly Ebele jumped out of bed.

In ten years' time my parents will be sixty.

Earlier today my teacher gave me detention.

In a very silly way Ciaran skipped across the yard.

In the kitchen there's a present for you.

2 Put a tick next to the sentences which use commas correctly and put a cross next to the ones that don't use them correctly.

Before dawn, everything is very peaceful.

In Italy pizza and pasta, are very popular foods.

As quickly as possible, he packed his bags.

Under the new rules, we can't wear jewellery to school.

Last week the boys, won the football match.

Rewrite the incorrect sentences with commas in the right places.

....

....

Section 8 — Commas

3 Rewrite these sentences with commas in the correct places.

Before school Kim made her packed lunch.

....

On Tuesday I am going to the cinema.

....

Every morning my mum runs 5 km.

....

In town there is a really big skate park.

....

4 Match each adverbial phrase to the correct main clause. Then write out the complete sentences. Remember to put commas in the correct places.

Adverbial Phrases	Main clauses
On the left	she crept through the house.
Every year	she set off for school.
Like a mouse	we visit my aunt.
Earlier than usual	you can see my old house.

1. ....

2. ....

3. ....

4. ....

Now Try This Underline the fronted adverbials in question 3. Use them to start four sentences of your own. Make sure you put commas in the correct places.

Section 8 — Commas

Commas for Extra Information

Commas can also be used to separate **extra information** in a sentence.

They go **either side** of the **extra information**.

The pupils, who had eaten lunch, went outside.

The sentence should still **make sense** when the **extra information** is **removed**.

1) Put a tick next to the sentences which use commas correctly and put a cross next to the ones that don't.

The flight, even though it felt really long, only took three hours.

My brothers who are twins, are called Eamon and Archie.

We saw, my teacher Mr Harris, in the park.

Dr Grey, our family doctor, told me to try to get more sleep.

Rewrite the incorrect sentences with commas in the right places.

....

....

....

2) Add commas in the correct places in the sentences below.

On Thursday the day after tomorrow I am going on holiday. I am going with my two sisters Izzy and Amelia and our mum. We're spending a few days in Portugal a really hot country before flying back to England. The holiday which was quite expensive should be really fun.

Section 8 — Commas

3 **Rewrite** each sentence with the commas in the **correct** places.

The charity auction which raised hundreds of pounds was a great success.

....

....

Pepperoni my favourite pizza topping is a kind of sausage.

....

....

The shepherd who'd lost all his sheep was very upset.

....

....

4 **Rewrite** the sentences below, adding the **extra information** in the boxes. Use **commas** where they are needed.

Charles Dickens was born in 1812. [a famous English writer]

....

....

My pet mice are adorable. [called Sammy and Sally]

....

....

My parents get on really well. [who met fifteen years ago]

....

....

Now Try This — Write three sentences. Use commas to add extra information to each one.

Section 8 — Commas

Comma Practice

Use **commas** to make **lists**, avoid **confusion**, after **subordinate clauses**, after **fronted adverbials** and for **extra information**.

Next week, let's play golf.

Ife, my friend, is very tall.

I'm going to draw, Evie.

When I find it, we can go home.

You can have chips, mash or rice.

1) Put a tick next to the sentences that <u>use commas correctly</u> and put a cross next to the sentences that <u>don't</u>.

The Alps, a European mountain range, are popular with skiers. ☐

The bus stops on King Street Russel Lane and Victoria Square. ☐

At the beach, I had an ice cream and read my book. ☐

The book, about electricity looks, quite difficult. ☐

In England the weather, is often grey and cloudy. ☐

Even if, I knew it I wouldn't tell you the answer. ☐

My favourite fruits are apples, oranges, pears and strawberries. ☐

Mrs Williams, our window cleaner, fell off her ladder yesterday. ☐

Rewrite the <u>incorrect</u> sentences with <u>commas</u> in the right places.

....

....

....

....

....

Section 8 — Commas

2) Underline the subordinate clauses and add commas where needed.

Many people came to the fair <u>until it started to rain</u>.

<u>While she was shopping</u>, we prepared her surprise.

<u>Even though I love most fruits</u>, I hate apples.

<u>If I get home in time</u>, I'll start making our tea.

<u>Although the pirate was very scary</u>, her parrot was hilarious.

You can help me with the decorations <u>since you're so early</u>.

<u>Provided that you've brought your trunks</u>, we can go swimming today.

You can't go to football practice <u>unless you've done your homework</u>.

Remember — a subordinate clause doesn't make sense on its own.

3) Explain how adding or moving a comma changes the meaning of these sentences.

In the town square, people were looking at the shops.

In the town, square people were looking at the shops.

....

....

....

My least favourite things about school are history teachers and detention.

My least favourite things about school are history, teachers and detention.

....

....

....

Now Try This — Write five sentences about your favourite place.
You should use commas for a different reason in each sentence.

Section 9 — Brackets and Dashes

Brackets for Extra Information

Brackets are used to **separate extra information** from the rest of a sentence.
You always need a **pair** of brackets — never use one on its own.

> Uncle Nigel (my dad's older brother) works on a farm.

The bit inside the brackets is the **extra information**.
The **rest** of the sentence would still **make sense** without it.

The extra information is sometimes called a parenthesis.

1) Put a <u>tick</u> next to the sentences that use brackets <u>correctly</u>.

Rhinos (an endangered species) mostly live in Africa. ☐

Umaru was late to work yesterday (Tuesday). ☐

The competition was won by Mr Fairclough (a train driver). ☐

Chris was upset (at the result) they should have won. ☐

Abi's dress pink with white flowers (was too long). ☐

Our neighbour (Mrs Bewley) forgot to put the bins out. ☐

2) In each of these sentences there is <u>one</u> bracket in the <u>incorrect</u> position. Cross it out and write a <u>new</u> bracket in the <u>correct</u> position.

Our friends James (and Alun) live across the road.

(When we went fishing last weekend), I caught nothing.

It was too hot (thirty-six degrees for the cat) to go outside.

The majority of us (seventy-five) per cent wanted Fraser to win.

Agata and Akhil our (aunt and uncle) gave us a new sofa.

3 Each of these sentences only has one bracket.
Put the missing one in the correct box.

The portrait (painted [ ] in 1839 [ ] cost Mr Dough a lot of money.

Fatima [ ] finished her knitting [ ] a woolly jumper).

There are eleven players (including a goalkeeper [ ] in a hockey [ ] team.

Logan's tie [ ] black [ ] with sparkly bits) had a hole [ ] in it.

4 Add brackets to the sentences below in the correct positions.

Jenny and Barbara the identical twins work at the same shop .

Arthur Coddle an English author wrote several novels .

The café is closed on Mondays the manager's day off .

'The Rising Sea' my favourite book is about mermaids .

The poodle a breed of dog has lots of fur .

5 Complete each of these sentences by writing your own phrase in the gaps between the brackets.

The main course (..) was delicious.

Hazel's dog (..) likes to chase tennis balls.

The workers (..) didn't turn up for work.

Indira's favourite toy (..) was very old.

Rodney's car (..) pulled up outside.

The supermarket (..) is overrun by mice.

Now Try This Write a simple sentence. Then, rewrite your sentence three times, adding a different piece of extra information in brackets each time.

Section 9 — Brackets and Dashes

Dashes for Extra Information

A **pair of dashes** can also **separate extra information** in a sentence.

> Mason — the builder — arrived before Nathan.

The dashes go **around** the extra bit of information.

1 Put a cross next to the sentence which has used dashes <u>incorrectly</u>. Then rewrite this sentence adding dashes <u>correctly</u>.

Gary left his hat — by accident — on top of the car. ☐

We built — a sandcastle a big one — on the beach. ☐

Alex's cat — the one with the stripy tail — eats biscuits. ☐

The girls — especially Sonal and Ailsa — love the sunshine. ☐

....

....

2 <u>Add</u> dashes <u>correctly</u> to the passage below.

Mr Miller the county's finest baker has announced his plans to bake Britain's first gingerbread hotel. The hotel four storeys high will open next summer. Six thousand people many from the local area have applied to stay at the hotel during the first month. Mr Miller's son also a baker will be in charge of the construction of the hotel. Two tonnes of ginger grown specially by Mr Miller will be used in the project. Tim Bury a famous architect thinks that the plan will simply not work.

3

One of the dashes in each sentence is in the **wrong** place.
Rewrite each sentence putting it in the **right** place.

Moussa — and Sonny — the carpenters need some new tools.

....

There is a box of chocolates — a big box in the — kitchen.

....

Adam — forgot his lunch yet again — this morning.

....

Hayley a famous comedian — is performing — tonight.

....

4

Rewrite each of these sentences in the correct order using a pair of dashes.

| my cat | likes to eat tuna | a tabby |

....

| is in the opera | a talented singer | Lea's mum |

....

| a type of ride | the waltzer | makes me dizzy |

....

Now Try This: "My sister a doctor is coming to visit at the weekend."
Where should the dashes go in this sentence? How can you tell?

Section 9 — Brackets and Dashes

Section 10 — Apostrophes

Apostrophes for Missing Letters

Use an apostrophe to show where you've left letters out of a shortened word.

you are → you're   might have → might've   will not → won't

Sometimes the shortened word doesn't quite match the words it's made from.

1) Shorten these words using an apostrophe.

she will → ....   they are → ....

they have → ....   where is → ....

who would → ....   that will → ....

he is → ....   must not → ....

2) Write a sentence using shortened versions of the words below.

should have

....

might have

....

will not

....

could have

....

Now Try This: Write a sentence that uses some words that can be shortened. Then, rewrite the sentence using the shortened versions of those words.

Apostrophes for Single Possession

To show that someone or something owns something, add an apostrophe and 's'. For singular nouns, you always add the 's', even if the word ends in 's' already.

apostrophe + 's'   the cook's pot   the walrus's tusks   apostrophe + 's'

1 Complete these phrases by writing out the word in the box to show possession.

fox	→ the ....fox's.... fur	Jess	→ .... brother
puppy	→ our .... bed	kite	→ the .... tail
bus	→ the .... seats	pot	→ the .... lid

2 Add an apostrophe and 's' to these sentences to show possession.

Miss Ellenby class had all got new school bags for the new year. Rosie bag was covered in dinosaurs. Ahmed bag was bright red and had his favourite band faces on it. Robin bag had more pockets than Miss Ellenby said he could ever need!

3 Write a sentence about each picture that uses an apostrophe and an 's' to show possession.

....

....

Now Try This Describe what a friend is wearing using apostrophes to show possession.

Section 10 — Apostrophes

Apostrophes for Plural Possession

You can use apostrophes to show possession for plural nouns.

the fairies' castle

If a plural noun ends in 's', you only add an apostrophe.

the men's room

If a plural noun doesn't end in 's', add an apostrophe and an 's'.

1 Cross out the phrases which don't use apostrophes correctly.

belonging to the frogs →	~~the frogs's~~	the frogs'
belonging to the sisters →	the sisters's	the sisters'
belonging to the women →	the women's	the womens'
belonging to the birds →	the birds's	the birds'
belonging to the mice →	the mice's	the mices'

2 Using an apostrophe or an apostrophe and an 's', write down what each group of people or things has.

The flowers have pink petals. ...The flowers' petals are pink...

The students have heavy books. ....

The dice have black spots. ....

The guitars have metal strings. ....

The children have blue bricks. ....

The owls have big eyes. ....

Now Try This — "The girls stories were always about her toys adventures." Where should the apostrophes go to show that this sentence is about one girl and two toys?

Section 10 — Apostrophes

Its and It's

The words 'its' and 'it's' mean two different things.

its — This means 'belonging to it'. → the cat licked its paw

it's — This means 'it is' or 'it has'. → it's raining   it's been great

1) Tick the sentences which use 'its' or 'it's' correctly and cross the sentences that use them incorrectly.

It's fun to travel abroad. ☐   It's my birthday today. ☐

Its got to work this time. ☐   The lion chased its prey. ☐

The panda ate it's dinner. ☐   Its time to go home now. ☐

It's taken no time at all. ☐   The baby threw its toys. ☐

Write out the incorrect sentences using 'its' or 'it's' correctly.

....

....

....

2) Write 'Its' or 'It's' to complete the sentences below.

.... not dark outside yet.   .... sign is falling down.

.... stripes are black and white.   .... the busiest shop in town.

.... park has a jungle gym.   .... home is under the floor.

.... important to eat fruit.   .... got to be finished later.

Now Try This — "The horse decided to exchange it's purple hat for a green one."
Explain why it is incorrect to use 'it's' in this sentence.

Section 10 — Apostrophes

Apostrophe Practice

You can use apostrophes to show where letters are missing, or to show possession for nouns. Remember that 'its' and 'it's' are two different words.

1) Shorten these words using apostrophes.

what will → .... who is → ....

are not → .... when has → ....

you would → .... does not → ....

2) Fill in the missing gaps with the short and long versions of the words.

is not	....
....	where'll
why is	....
have not	....
....	might've

....	let's
....	hasn't
we would	....
....	he's
should not	....

3) Add apostrophes to the underlined words below, if they are needed.

My <u>hamsters</u> name is Hector, and <u>Ive</u> had him for two years.

The shark showed <u>its</u> teeth and swam towards the <u>fishermans</u> boat.

<u>Its</u> been a great day, but now the park is shutting <u>its</u> gates.

<u>Dinas</u> going to her <u>dads</u> house tomorrow because <u>its</u> Wednesday.

Section 10 — Apostrophes

4 Rewrite each phrase so that it changes from singular to plural.

singular	plural
The pig's dirty snout →	The pigs' dirty snouts
The car's old engine →	
The woman's red coat →	
The dress's thin straps →	
The tiger's sharp claws →	
The man's good work →	

5 Draw lines to match each phrase to its correct meaning.

- the girl's cats — one girl owns one cat
- the girls' cats — one girl owns two cats
- the girl's cat — two girls own one cat
- the girls' cat — two girls own two cats

6 Write two sentences about the picture, one using 'its' and one using 'it's'.

....

....

Now Try This: Write a short passage about a family member. Make sure your passage uses apostrophes to shorten words and show possession.

Section 10 — Apostrophes

Section 11 — Inverted Commas

Punctuating Speech

Speech always **ends** with a **punctuation mark**, which goes **inside** the speech marks.

If speech starts **part-way through** the **sentence**, you need to add a **comma before** the speech.

Morven said, "Is he ill?"

Speech always **starts** with a **capital letter**, even when it isn't at the start of the sentence.

1) Put <u>inverted commas</u> (speech marks) in the <u>correct places</u> in the sentences below.

Fred said happily , This is going to be the best weekend ever .

Rachel , stop that at once ! shouted her aunt .

Please may I buy some sweets to take home ? asked Hannah .

Arundhati said , We need to take a packed lunch with us today .

I want to go and see the tigers first , said Anna excitedly .

2) <u>Circle</u> the <u>punctuation mistake</u> in <u>each sentence</u>, then <u>draw a line</u> to show <u>what</u> the mistake is.

"I don't have any crayons", said Bishan.

"Are you going to the party"? asked Mirek.

Dad shouted, "dinner is ready!"

Emily said "I have a baby brother."

"I'm practising all the time", said Max.

"This cookie is delicious" said Sophie.

My sister asked, "is this your skirt?"

Nasreen shouted "Come here please!"

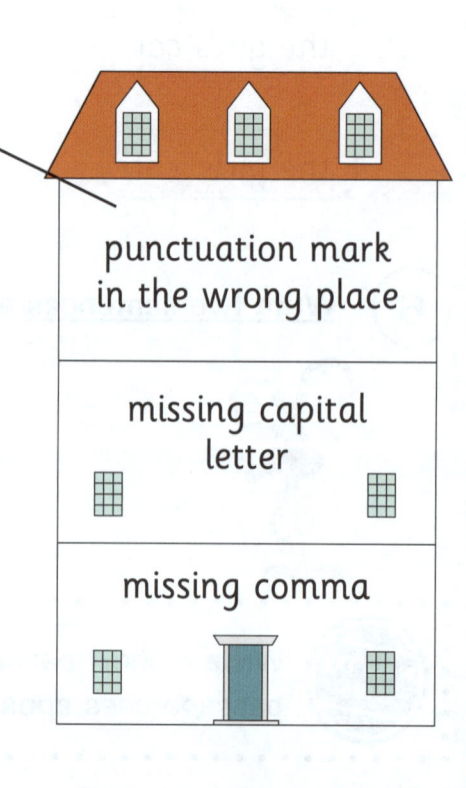

- punctuation mark in the wrong place
- missing capital letter
- missing comma

3 Put the correct punctuation marks into the boxes to complete the sentences.

The children shouted [,] "We love Grantham School Hockey Team [!] "

"Today I am going to talk about my hobby [,] " said Nicholas [.]

["] What are we going to do with this monkey [?] " asked Molly.

["] Have you got your passport and your ticket [?] " my aunt asked.

Yasmin yelled [,] "I can see the theme park over there [!] "

"Can we change the channel, please [?] " asked Yusif [.]

4 Rewrite each sentence using inverted commas and the correct punctuation.

I don't feel very well at all said Harry

....

Shufen asked How do I get to the station

....

There's a fire in the gym yelled William

....

5 Use the words below to write a sentence that includes inverted commas.

asked   football   score

....

....

Now Try This Think of a conversation you recently had with a friend. Write some sentences of speech to show what you both said.

Punctuating Speech in Two Parts

Sometimes speech is broken up by other information.

The sentence hasn't finished yet, so you need a comma.

"Look," said Thu, "it's there!"

You still need a comma before the second bit of speech...

You don't need a capital letter if the second bit of speech is part of the same sentence.

...and punctuation at the end.

1) Tick the sentences which are punctuated correctly.

"At long last," said the villain, "the whole world will be mine!" ☐

"That piano over there" said Mr Davidson "needs to be tuned." ☐

"I like apple crumble", said Imogen, "but I prefer blueberry". ☐

"Excuse me," said the lady, "do you know what time it starts?" ☐

2) Put the punctuation in the boxes into each of the sentences. The punctuation is already in the correct order.

" , " , " . " → This drink said Cerys tastes of nothing

" , " , " . " → I think said Rob it's just round here

" , " , " ! " → And then said Sam he just disappeared

3) Rewrite each sentence using inverted commas and the correct punctuation.

I think said Gwen that we should all go

....

Just focus said Nia and it will be fine

....

Now Try This: Rewrite this sentence so that the speech is broken up into two parts:
"That duck is wearing boots and it's juggling," exclaimed Rupa.

Section 11 — Inverted Commas

Section 12 — Paragraphs and Layout

Paragraphs

Paragraphs are used to show when a new **subject**, **place** or **time** is introduced. You also need to start a new paragraph when a **new person speaks**.

1 Write a <u>sentence</u> that would go in the <u>same paragraph</u> as the <u>sentences below</u>.

> Computers are useful for lots of different things. → ....

> Last week I went horse riding for the first time. → ....

2 Use paragraph markers (//) to break the following passage into <u>three paragraphs</u>.

On Tuesday, I was playing outside with my friend Mia. She is a great skateboarder. I don't have a skateboard of my own, so I asked Mia if I could have a go on hers. I really wanted to practise. "No," said Mia, "you're not as good as me so you might break it." Last year, Mia got eight chocolate eggs for Easter but she wouldn't let anyone else have any. I don't think Mia is very good at sharing.

Give a <u>reason</u> for starting each <u>new paragraph</u>.

2nd paragraph ....

3rd paragraph ....

3 Put paragraph markers (//) into this passage to show where new paragraphs should start.

"This is hopeless," moaned Ashling, "I can't do it."

The maths exercise had taken her most of the lesson already. "It's easy," said Jack. "You're forgetting to add the seven, that's all." Ashling wasn't impressed. She covered the page with her arms and scowled at him.

"Don't worry, Jack," said Tracy. "Ashling never lets anyone help."

Rewrite the passage, starting new paragraphs where you marked them above.

....

....

....

....

....

....

....

....

Now Try This What are the four reasons why you should start a new paragraph?

Section 12 — Paragraphs and Layout

Headings and Subheadings

Headings and subheadings help with presentation and structure. They are a good way of organising information.

1) Draw lines to match the headings to the correct type of text.

- Welcome to Paradise
- A Treat for Your Taste Buds
- More Than Just Books

- A review of a local restaurant
- A leaflet promoting the library
- An advert for a luxury holiday

2) Write a subheading for each of the following paragraphs.

A Happy Future at Tattlefinch High

....

At Tattlefinch High we employ the highest quality teachers across all departments so that your child receives the best education.

....

Our extracurricular programme provides something for every child to enjoy, from trampolining to textiles and cross-country running to cookery.

....

Thanks to a generous grant, we have a brand-new IT room attached to the library and an interactive whiteboard in every single classroom.

Now Try This: Write a fourth paragraph about Tattlefinch High and give it a subheading.

Section 13 — Prefixes

Prefixes – 'under', 'over', 'en' and 'em'

A prefix is a letter or group of letters that can be added to the beginning of a word to make a new word.

'load' is the root word.

'over-' is a prefix. → over + load → overload

The spelling of the root word does not change when a prefix is added. Prefixes can tell us useful information about a root word.

'over-' means 'over' or 'too much'   'under-' means 'under' or 'too little'

1) Add over- or under- to the sentences below so that they make sense.

I .... slept today and was nearly late for school.

Our garden looks a mess — it's so .... grown.

Work was stressful today because we were .... staffed.

Deserts are usually .... populated areas of the world.

I hate it when trains are .... crowded.

Asma doesn't have the skills for the job — she's .... qualified.

2) Sort the letters below into the right order to spell a root word. Add over- and under- to the word to make two new words.

root word   new words

a p i d

e v a u l

The prefixes 'en-' and 'em-' can sometimes mean 'to put into'.

'Em' is used instead of 'en' when the root word starts with a 'b' or 'p'.

'em' is the prefix. → embrace ← 'brace' is a root word which starts with 'b'.

3 Add en- or em- to complete each word correctly.

..........bolden   ....courage   ....act

..........rage   ....pathise   ....power

..........danger   ....circle   ....force

4 Use the clues to work out each word beginning with en- or em-.

make larger → [ ][ ][l][ ][ ][g][ ]

[ ][ ][l][ ][v][ ][ ] ← make lively

make bitter → [ ][ ][b][ ][ ][t][ ][ ]

[ ][ ][ ][c][ ][ ][s][ ][ ] ← to surround

5 Write three sentences, each using one of the words below.

oversized

....

underrated

....

entangled

....

Now Try This: Use a dictionary to find ten words that start with 'under', 'over', 'en' or 'em'.

Prefixes – 'mid', 'pre', 'fore' and 'non'

Prefixes can tell us useful information about a root word.

'mid-' means 'middle'.   'pre-' and 'fore-' mean 'before'.   'non-' means 'not'.

midfield   preview   forethought   nonadjustable

1 Circle the prefixes in the sentences below.

Remember — when you add a prefix, the spelling of the root word does not change.

The midterm test will take place on Tuesday.

If you would like to take part, you need to preregister.

The problem with pollution is at the forefront of the agenda.

2 Fill in the gaps in the words below using the correct prefixes from the box.

mid-   pre-   fore-   non-

..................mature   ....head   ....fiction

..................ground   ....date   ....way

..................summer   ....week   ....program

3 Complete the words in these sentences using mid-, pre-, fore- or non-.

Fortune tellers believe they can .... see what will happen in the future.

To make sure we get a seat, we had better .... book our tickets.

Cara always has a .... morning snack at her desk at work.

Barack was disappointed that he had ordered a .... refillable drink.

The cricketer caught the ball in .... air to win the match for his team.

A pink stretch limo pulled up in the .... court of the house.

4 Circle the **correct** spelling of each word to complete the sentences below.

The weather midcast / <u>forecast</u> for the weekend looks awful.

Cheryl loves football — she's a great <u>midfielder</u> / forefielder.

The presection / <u>midsection</u> of the boat sprang a leak.

The toddlers play happily together at nonschool / <u>preschool</u>.

All the animals take a nap at <u>midday</u> / preday to avoid the heat of the sun.

Forewinter / <u>Midwinter</u> in the jungle is still very hot.

Three long distance runners were nonselected / <u>preselected</u> for the Olympics.

I'm looking forward to a quick foreview / <u>preview</u> of my friend's new film.

5 <u>One</u> word is spelt with the <u>wrong prefix</u> in each of the sentences below. Rewrite the sentences on the dotted lines so that <u>all</u> the words are spelt <u>correctly</u>.

The jungle ball ends at forenight with fireworks.

....

I can't understand my little brother — he speaks presense.

....

Crocodiles look like nonhistoric creatures.

....

The workers received instructions from the midman.

....

The children were at the prepoint of the project.

....

Now Try This Choose five words from question 2 and use each one in a sentence.

Hyphenating Prefixes

Hyphens are used to **join words** together or **add** a **prefix**. Some words are written with hyphens so they **aren't confused** with similar words.

I re-sorted my papers.   I resorted to walking to work.

're-sorted' means 'to **sort again**'. It needs a hyphen to show that it means something **different** from 'resorted' which means 'to **turn to an undesirable option**'.

Hyphens are often used if the prefix ends in a **vowel** and the root word begins with a **vowel**. → co-own

1) Underline the prefixes in the words below.
Then rewrite the words with a hyphen in the correct place.

reexamine .... reemerge ....

proAmerican .... preorder ....

coordinate .... coexist ....

2) Hyphens have been added incorrectly to the words below.
Rewrite these words on the clipboard below with a hyphen in the correct place.

preo-wn

antiage-ing

reel-ect   reen-ter

proEuro-pean

antiAmer-ican

coow-ner

Section 13 — Prefixes

3 Circle the correct spelling of each word to complete the sentences below.

Samira re-sent / resent her letter to the mayor after receiving no reply.

Brad didn't re-sent / resent the fact that Stu beat him in the 100 m hurdles.

Many people are against the government's plans for reform / re-form.

The synchronised swimmers re-formed / reformed to create a heart shape.

Henry used invisible ink by mistake, so he had to resign / re-sign the form.

Julie had an argument with her boss and decided to resign / re-sign.

After mixing up the documents, we had to re-sort / resort them.

We had to re-sort / resort to pushing our car to the garage.

4 Add a prefix and a hyphen to the root words below so the sentences make sense.

I help my friends as much as possible — it's good to ....operate.

Kasia and Rhys are ....authors of a best-selling novel.

No one applied for the job, so the position will be ....advertised.

5 Write a sentence using each of the following words.

co-operation

....

anti-slavery

....

Now Try This Look at the words in question 3. How many more words can you think of where adding a hyphen makes a new word with a different meaning?

Section 13 — Prefixes

Section 14 — Word Endings and Suffixes

Word Endings – The 'shun' Sound

When it comes at the end of words, the 'shun' sound can be spelt in different ways.

fiction   expansion   admission   optician

'-tion' is used when the root word ends in 't' or 'te'.   act → action

'-cian' is used when the root word ends in 'c' or 'cs'.   clinic → clinician

1) Underline the words below that are spelt incorrectly. Then write the correct spellings on the dotted lines.

'cian' is often used for occupations e.g. 'physician'.

mencian   hesitacian   politician   attencian   reduction   beautition   direction   physician   conversation   population

....
....
....
....

2) Draw lines from the word beginnings to the correct word endings.

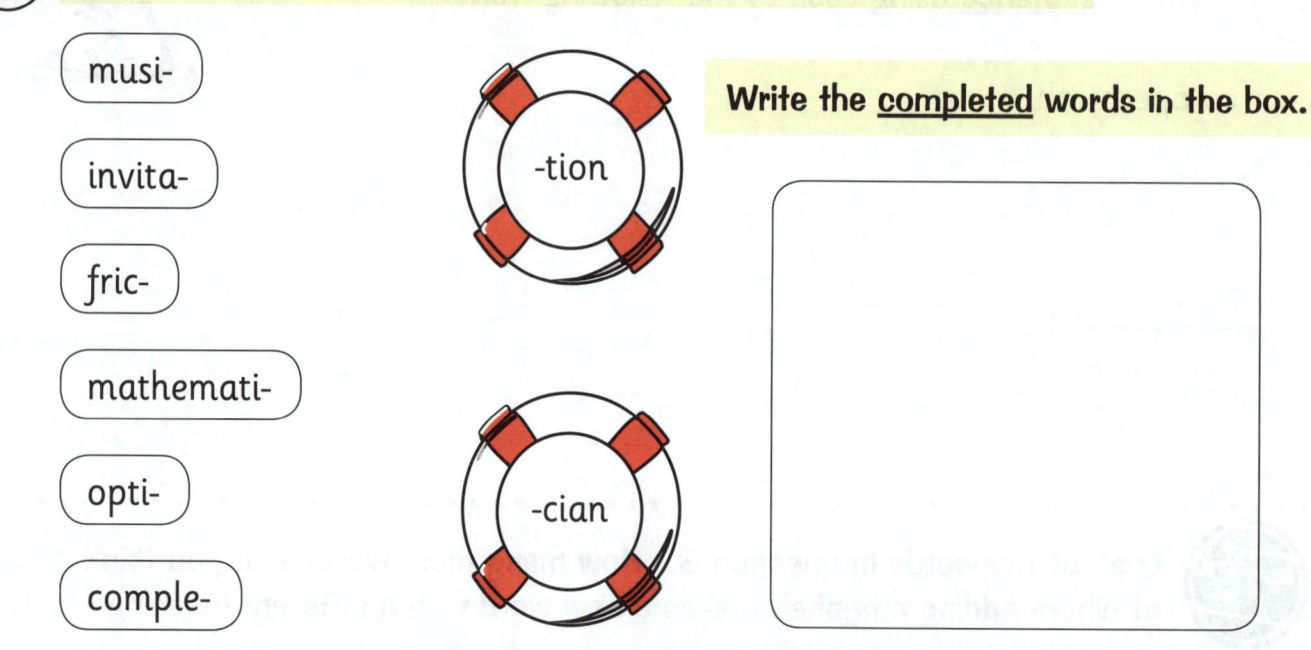

musi-
invita-
fric-
mathemati-
opti-
comple-

-tion

-cian

Write the completed words in the box.

'-sion' is usually used when the root word ends in 'd', 'de' or 'se'.

televise ➡ television

'-ssion' is used when the root word ends in 'ss' or 'mit'.

discuss ➡ discussion

Careful — there are some exceptions to this rule.

3 Complete the words in these sentences using -sion or -ssion.

It was a good deci.................. to go to on holiday.

Our car hit a tree — it was a terrible colli.................. .

The teacher gave me permi.................. to leave class early.

There was ten.................. between the football fans after the match.

He came to the conclu.................. that he should do more exercise.

It's an intru.................. into my private life when my sister reads my letters.

4 Use the clues to work out each word ending in a 'shun' sound.

something you intend to do ➡ | i | n | | | | | | |

a person who can do magic ➡ | m | a | | | | | | |

a talk ➡ | d | i | s | | | | | |

something you might go to hospital for ➡ | o | p | | | | | | |

a person who works with electricity ➡ | e | l | | | | | | |

an answer to a problem ➡ | s | o | | | | | | |

Now Try This How many of the words from question 4 can you use in a single sentence?

Section 14 — Word Endings and Suffixes

Word Endings – The 'shus' Sound

When it comes at the end of words, the 'shus' sound can be spelt in different ways.

gracious   cautious

If the root word ends in '-ce', the 'shus' sound is usually spelt '-cious'.

space → spacious

1) Fill in the missing letter to finish each word correctly.

overcau....ious   suspi....ious   cons....ious   atro....ious

2) Circle the words in the box below that are spelt correctly. Then, fill in the gaps in the sentences using the words that you circled.

delicious / delitious   vicious / vitious
precious / pretious   ficticious / fictitious

Terry tells lies — his stories are ....

Sharks can be .... creatures.

Dot thinks sprouts and cabbages are ....

Margery's jewellery is very .... to her.

3) Write a sentence using each of the following words.

ambitious

....

nutritious

....

Now Try This: List as many words ending in 'cious' and 'tious' as you can in two minutes.

Word Endings – The 'shul' Sound

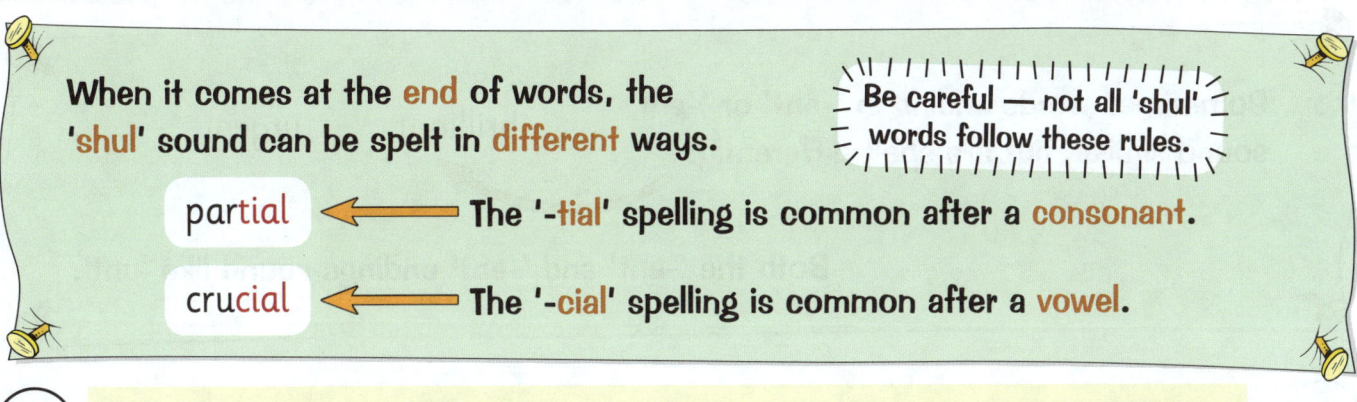

When it comes at the end of words, the 'shul' sound can be spelt in different ways.

Be careful — not all 'shul' words follow these rules.

partial ← The '-tial' spelling is common after a consonant.

crucial ← The '-cial' spelling is common after a vowel.

1) Circle the correct spelling of each word to complete the sentences below.

The local bakery had a spetial / **special** offer on their cakes.

My sister has the **potential** / potencial to be a pop star.

Darcey's **initial** / inicial response shocked the audience.

Our personal data should be kept **confidential** / confidencial.

2) Write each of these words with the correct 'shul' ending.

mar- → .... essen- → ....

artifi- → .... so- → ....

substan- → .... influen- → ....

3) Sort the letters below into the right order to spell a word ending in a 'shul' sound.

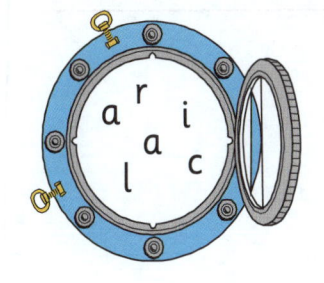

Letters: a, r, i, a, c, l → ....cial

Letters: a, i, p, a, c, l, s → ....cial

Letters: r, p, t, a, i, al → ....tial

Now Try This: Write three sentences using 'shul' words that aren't on this page.

Section 14 — Word Endings and Suffixes

Word Endings – 'ant' and 'ent'

Sometimes words ending in '-ant' or '-ent' sound similar, but are spelt differently.

brilliant   urgent

Both the '-ant' and '-ent' endings sound like 'unt'.

1 Put a tick in the boxes next to the words that are spelt correctly.
Put a cross in the boxes next to the words that are spelt incorrectly.

independent ☐   arrogent ☐   instrumant ☐

innocent ☐   hesitent ☐   expectent ☐

Write the correct spellings of the words you put a cross next to in the box below.

[   ]

2 Add -ant or -ent to spell the words below correctly.
Then write the completed words in the correct columns in the table.

mom..........
relev..........
toler..........
perman..........
evid..........
dist..........
tal..........

ant	ent

Section 14 — Word Endings and Suffixes

3 Some of the words in this passage are spelt incorrectly.
Circle the incorrect words and write the correct versions in the box below.

My friend Shingo made an interesting commant yesterday — he said that he's found a vacent plot of land owned by an independant building company. Shingo wants to build a house on the land, but he can't because the land is in fact an anciant burial site and archaeologists want to investigate the area.

4 Solve the clues to complete the crossword.

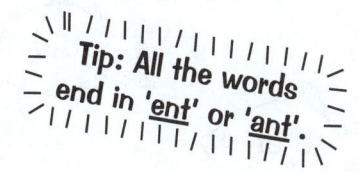

Tip: All the words end in 'ent' or 'ant'.

Across
1. An animal with a trunk
2. A remark

Down
1. If you don't do something on purpose, it's an...
2. When something doesn't make a sound, it's...
3. If it's a school day, but you're not at school, you are...
4. You might get one of these for your birthday or Christmas

Now Try This Write five sentences that include both a word ending in 'ant' and one ending 'ent'. Use different 'ant' and 'ent' words in each sentence.

Section 14 — Word Endings and Suffixes

Word Endings – 'ance', 'ancy' and 'ence', 'ency'

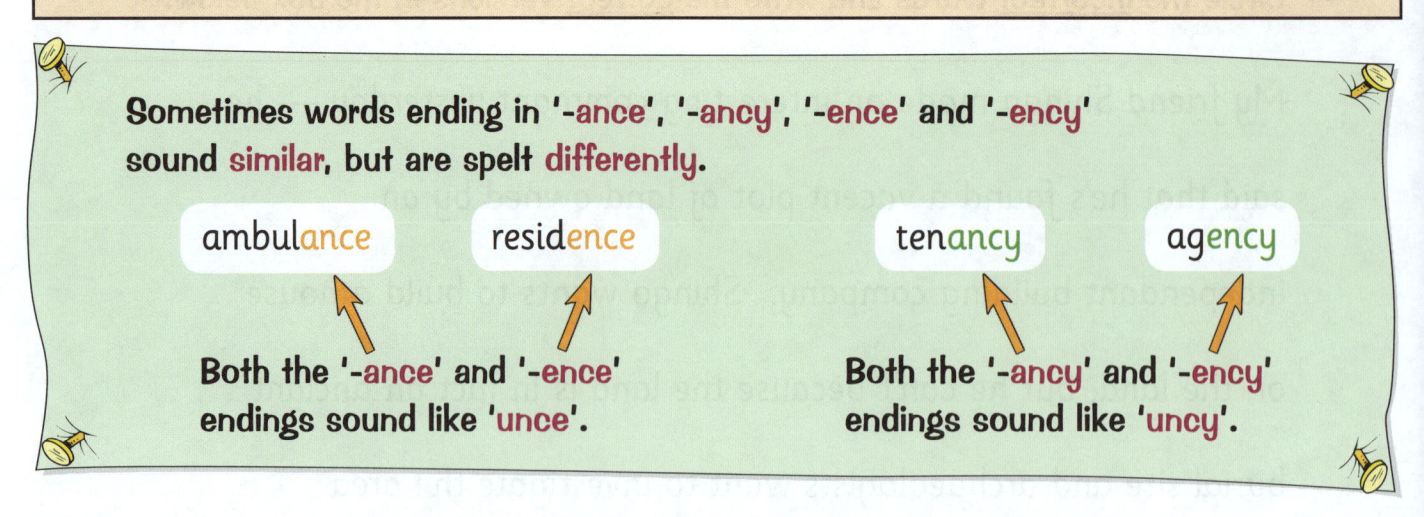

Sometimes words ending in '-ance', '-ancy', '-ence' and '-ency' sound similar, but are spelt differently.

ambulance   residence   tenancy   agency

Both the '-ance' and '-ence' endings sound like 'unce'.

Both the '-ancy' and '-ency' endings sound like 'uncy'.

1) Draw lines from the word beginnings to the correct word endings.

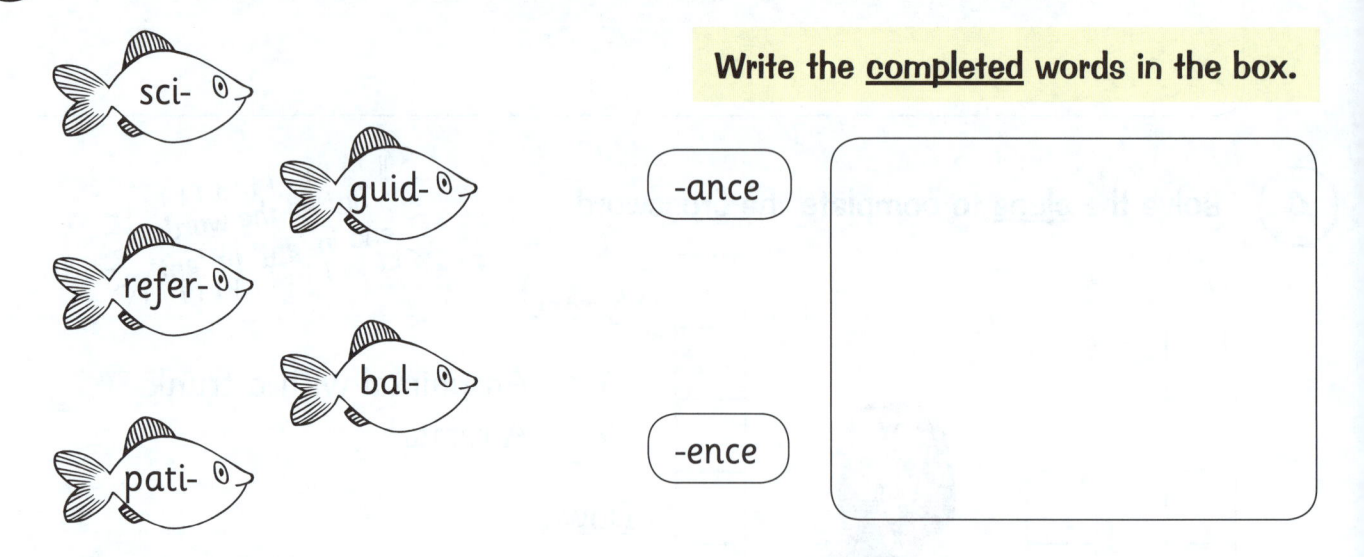

sci-
guid-
refer-
bal-
pati-

Write the completed words in the box.

-ance

-ence

2) Circle the correct spelling of each of the words in the sentences below.

Will didn't even have the decancy / decency to tell me he wasn't coming.

Paul has a high resistance / resistence to coughs and colds.

There was no evidance / evidence that the woman committed the crime.

TV can have a negative influance / influence on young viewers.

Navid completed the task with great efficiancy / efficiency.

There was great urgancy / urgency to repair the church roof.

The pupils' reliance / relience on spellcheckers worried the teacher.

Section 14 — Word Endings and Suffixes

3 Add -ance or -ence to spell the words below correctly. Then write the words out in full.

independ- + ... → ....

intellig- + ... → ....

subst- + ... → ....

experi- + ... → ....

4 Complete the words in these sentences using -ancy or -ency.

Huckleberry High School has a vac.............. for a new head teacher.

In an emerg.............., leave by the nearest exit.

Dogs can detect high frequ.............. sounds.

During her pregn.............., Helen's baby kicked a lot.

WANTED: New Head Teacher

Some people think women have a higher life expect.............. than men.

5 Read the clues, then choose the correctly spelt word from the box.

| performance | fragrence | currency | currancy |
| fragrance | absorbancy | absorbency | performence |

a play or a concert → ....

money → ....

a nice smell → ....

how much water a sponge can soak up → ....

Now Try This Write two sentences, using two words from question 5 in each one.

Section 14 — Word Endings and Suffixes

Word Endings – 'able', 'ible', 'ably' and 'ibly'

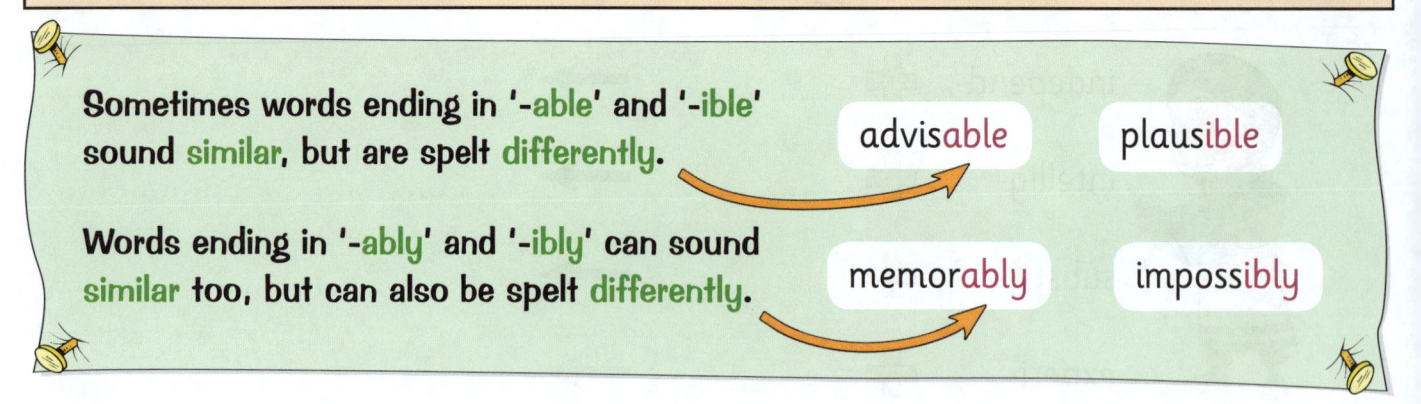

Sometimes words ending in '-able' and '-ible' sound similar, but are spelt differently.

advisable   plausible

Words ending in '-ably' and '-ibly' can sound similar too, but can also be spelt differently.

memorably   impossibly

1 Circle the correct spelling of each word to complete the sentences below.

Boris was <u>reasonably</u> / <u>reasonibly</u> tired after the long journey.

Coreen's new car has an <u>adjustable</u> / <u>adjustible</u> headrest.

Gymnasts need to be <u>flexable</u> / <u>flexible</u> to do their routines.

The hot air balloon was <u>incredably</u> / <u>incredibly</u> light.

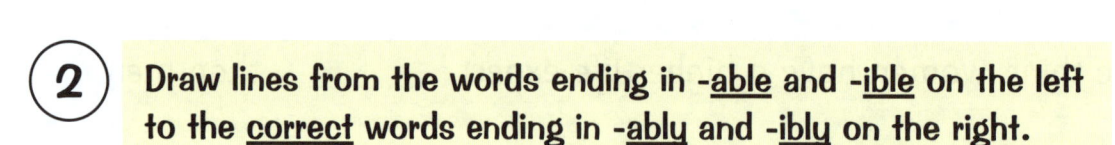

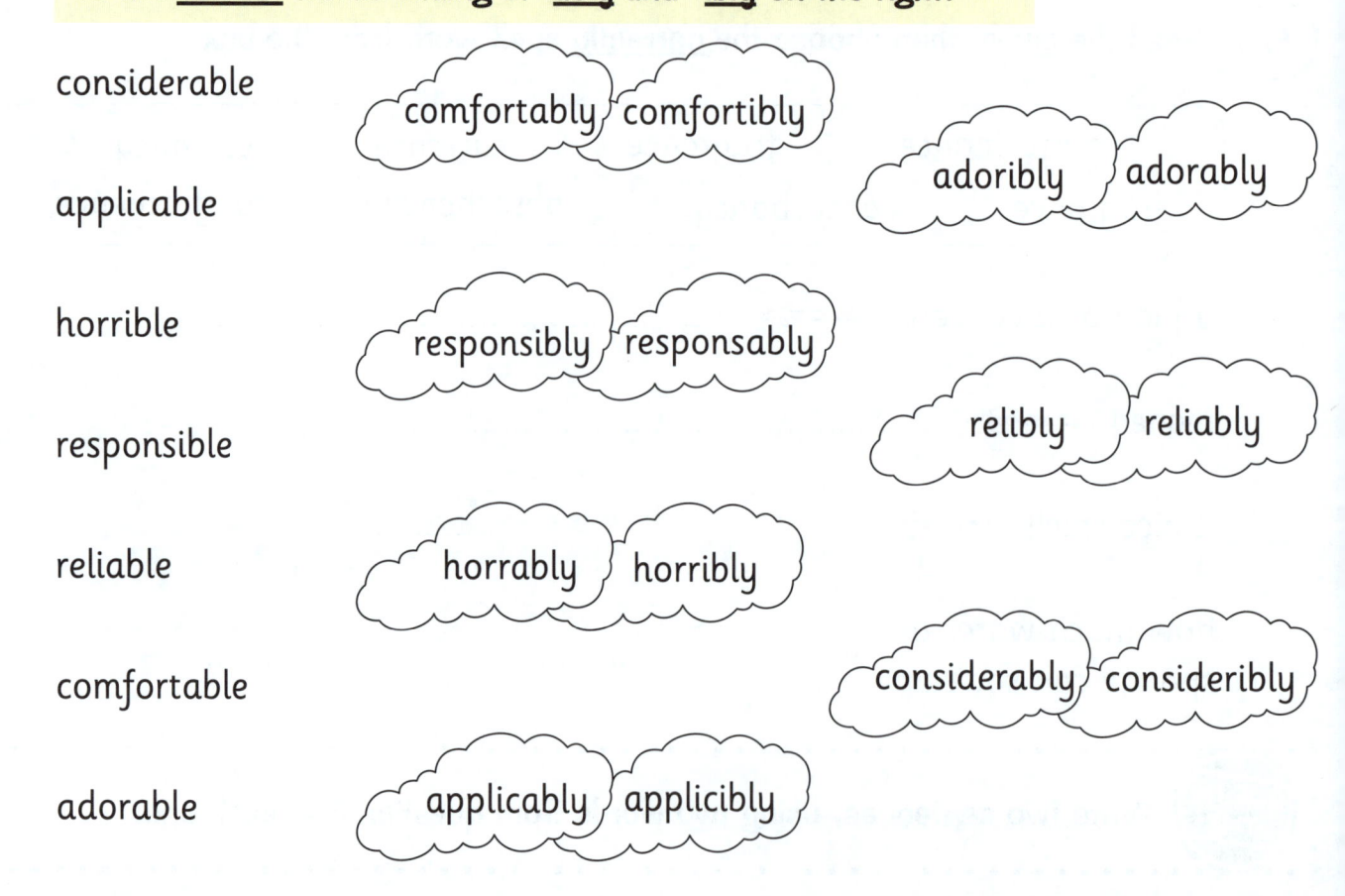

2 Draw lines from the words ending in -<u>able</u> and -<u>ible</u> on the left to the correct words ending in -<u>ably</u> and -<u>ibly</u> on the right.

considerable

applicable

horrible

responsible

reliable

comfortable

adorable

comfortably / comfortibly

adoribly / adorably

responsibly / responsably

relibly / reliably

horrably / horribly

considerably / consideribly

applicably / applicibly

Section 14 — Word Endings and Suffixes

3 Complete the words in these sentences using -<u>able</u>, -<u>ible</u>, -<u>ably</u> or -<u>ibly</u>.

The teacher said Felix's disruptive behaviour was not accept................. .

Today it was sunny, then rainy — the weather is so change................. .

The green mould on the icing made Kieron's cake ined................. .

During a fire drill, walk sens................. to the playing fields.

Rihanna's reason for being late was question................. .

Hamid was terr................. upset when everyone forgot his birthday.

The team was understand................. thrilled to win the match.

Neil miser................. parted with his teddy bear.

4 Write a <u>sentence</u> using each of the following words.

enjoyable

....

remarkably

....

visible

....

legibly

....

accessible

....

Now Try This: Write four sentences about what you would do if you met an alien. Use at least one word ending in 'able', 'ible', 'ably' or 'ibly' in each sentence.

Section 14 — Word Endings and Suffixes

Suffixes

A **suffix** is a letter or group of letters that can be **added** to the end of a **word** to make a **new word**.

'advert' is the root word. → advert + ise → advertise ← '-ise' is a suffix.

Sometimes the **spelling** of the root word **changes** when a **suffix** is **added**.

happy + ly → happily ← The 'y' in 'happy' **changes** to 'i' when the suffix '-ly' is added.

1) Add -<u>ous</u> or -<u>ly</u> to spell the words below correctly. Then write the words out in <u>full</u>.

Watch out — the <u>spelling</u> of some of these words needs to <u>change</u> when you add the <u>suffix</u>.

fame + ... → ....

angry + ... → ....

humour + ... → ....

scary + ... → ....

2) Put a <u>tick</u> in the boxes next to the words that are spelt <u>correctly</u>. Put a <u>cross</u> in the boxes next to the words that are spelt <u>incorrectly</u>.

simplify ☐   justiceify ☐   activeate ☐

memoryise ☐   criticise ☐   terrorify ☐

Write the <u>correct</u> spellings of the words you put a cross next to in the box below.

Section 14 — Word Endings and Suffixes

3

Draw lines to match the word beginnings to the correct suffix.

Nouns and adjectives often turn into verbs when suffixes are added to them.

summar

hyphen

advert

decor

class

Write the completed words in the box.

-ise   -ate   -ify

4

Complete the words in these sentences using -ate, -ise, or -ify.

The Prime Minister did not author............ Mr Smith to clean the bathroom.

I origin............ from Japan.

The pupils will not............ the teacher when they have completed their work.

Bruce and Violet are scientists — they special............ in human biology.

Travellers want to capital............ on cheap flights to Majorca.

5

Add the correct '-ise' or '-ify' ending to each of these word beginnings, then write the word in a sentence.

sympath............

....

horr............

....

apolog............

....

Now Try This — Think of four more words ending in '-ise' or '-ify'. Use each one in a sentence.

Section 14 — Word Endings and Suffixes

Section 15 — Confusing Words

'ei' and 'ie' Words

Use this rhyme to help you remember how to spell ei and ie words:

'i' before 'e' except after 'c' if the vowel sound rhymes with bee

piece ← Rhymes with bee, so 'i' before 'e'.

deceive ← Rhymes with bee but follows a 'c' — so 'e' before 'i'.

neighbour ← Doesn't rhyme with bee, so 'e' before 'i'.

scientist ← Doesn't rhyme with bee but follows a 'c' — so 'i' before 'e'.

1) Add the letters ie or ei to each of the words below, so that they match the pictures.

shr......k    sh......ld    f......ld    w......ght

2) Complete the words below using either 'ei' or 'ie'.

c......ling   pr......st   rec......ve   rel......ve

gr......f   bel......ve   conc......ve   dec......ve

3) Make an ie word out of the letters in each of the rubber rings.

Ring 1: p, c, e, i, e
Ring 2: t, h, i, e, f
Ring 3: c, e, h, i, f

....

**Some words don't follow the 'i before e' rule. → protein
You just have to learn these words.**

4) Fill in the gaps in the sentences below using the correct words from the box.

> relieved / releived   sieze / seize   neighbour / nieghbour   freind / friend

My best .... is called Emma.

Not all the words in the box are spelt correctly.

You will be .... to hear that we won.

We must .... this opportunity to improve our results.

Our .... complained that my violin practice was too loud.

5) Solve the clues below and then find the answers in the wordsearch.

Something found in tea and coffee

| C | | | | | | E | |

A piece of paper showing what you bought

| R | | | | | T |

A person who steals

| T | | | F | |

Your sister's daughter

| N | | | E |

If something doesn't take very long, it's

| B | | | F |

```
T E I M N I E C E
M H R E I S I A E
H T I R E I W F F
I E S E A B N F L
U I E C F D E E I
E H I E E H E I G
I V T I E I T N I
L E O P O R E E R
E W S T H T I I E
E U B R I E F A I
```

Now Try This: How many 'ei' and 'ie' words from these pages can you use in one paragraph?

Section 15 — Confusing Words

Words with 'ough' in

Words that contain the letters 'ough' can sound very different. For example:

Here the 'ough' letters sound like 'oh'. → though

through ← Here the 'ough' letters sound like 'oo'.

Here the 'ough' letters sound like 'off'. → cough

1 Draw lines to match each ough word with the correct sound.

- fought
- bough
- trough
- thought

'ow'
'or'
'off'

- cough
- sought
- nought
- plough

2 Put a tick in the boxes next to the ough words that have an 'uff' sound.

- tough ☐
- though ☐
- enough ☐
- dough ☐
- rough ☐
- bought ☐

3 Draw lines to link the ough words that rhyme.

bough   though   ought   thorough

borough   brought   dough   plough

Section 15 — Confusing Words

4) Solve the clues to find the ough words.

another word for but → a | l | | | | | |

what pigs eat out of → t | | | | |

another word for nothing or nil → n | | | | |

5) Fill in the gaps in the sentences below using the ough words in the box.

| throughout | enough | tough | bought | ought |

I've had .... of this album — can we change it?

Laura knew that she .... to visit her grandma more often.

.... her career, Becky had always tried her best.

Simon complained that his steak was far too ....

Niall .... his girlfriend a kitten for her birthday.

6) Write each of these words in a sentence.

through

....

thorough

....

though

....

Now Try This: Write three sentences, using a different 'ough' word in each one. The letters 'ough' should make a different sound in each word.

Section 15 — Confusing Words

Words with Silent Letters

Silent letters are letters that you don't hear when you say a word.

bomb   wreck   knock

The 'b', 'w' and 'k' are all silent letters in these words.

1) Circle the silent letters in each of the words below.

| exhaust | when | guess | know |
| listen | hour | knee | comb |

2) Add silent letters to each of the words, so that they match the pictures.

i ... land   lam ...   this ... le   si ... n   ca ... f   g ... ost

3) Draw lines to match the words with the silent letters they contain.

whirl — silent w — plumber

campaign — — write

limb — silent h — answer

gnome — silent g — wheat

sword — silent b — whistle

Section 15 — Confusing Words

4) Fill in the gaps in the sentences below using the correct words from the box.

> honest / onest   climbed / climed   nocked / knocked
> nife / knife   school / scool   sent / scent

Not all the words in the box are spelt correctly.

I .... on the door, but no one came.

Last year I .... Mount Everest.

I have to wear a yellow tie as part of my .... uniform.

You should always be careful when using a ....

I never lie — I am very ....

Detectives sometimes use dogs to follow a ....

5) Circle the correct spelling of each word to complete the sentences below.

Wednesday / Whensday is in the middle of the week.

I ofhen / often have fish and chips for tea.

I need to pay my dhet / debt off before I go on holiday.

We love playing in the autumn / authum leaves.

Estimate is another word for ghess / guess.

6) Write each of these words in a sentence.

crumb ➡ ....

knuckle ➡ ....

column ➡ ....

Now Try This — How many words with silent letters can you write down in two minutes?

Section 15 — Confusing Words

Unstressed Vowels

Unstressed vowels are vowel sounds that you can't hear clearly.

animal sounds like animul
Sometimes they sound like a **different vowel**.

factory sounds like factry
Sometimes they sound like they're **not there at all**.

1 Circle the unstressed vowel in each of the following words.

different	temperature	interesting	envelope
easily	personal	information	economical
frightening	fattening	offering	original

2 Circle the correct spelling of each word.

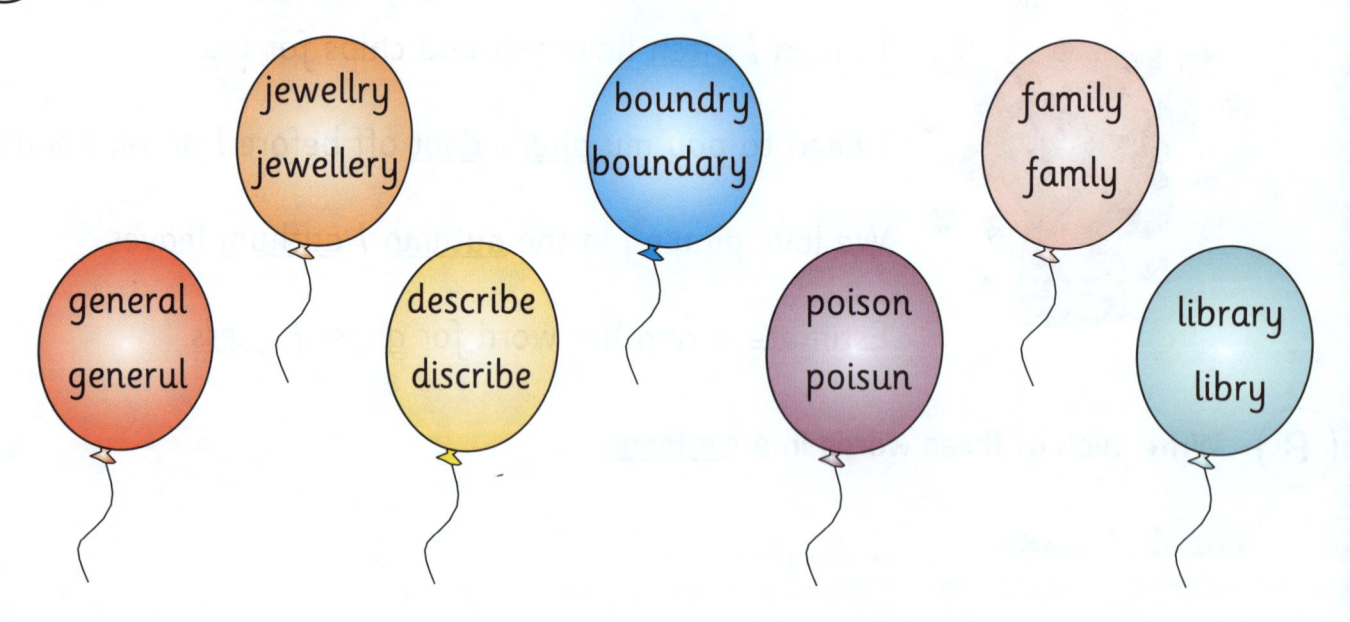

- jewellry / jewellery
- boundry / boundary
- family / famly
- general / generul
- describe / discribe
- poison / poisun
- library / libry

3 Complete these words using unstressed vowels.

refrig….rate   confid….nt   veg….table   mem….ry

doct….r   conc….ntrate   bus….ness   marv….llous

Section 15 — Confusing Words

4

Complete the words below by adding in the missing <u>unstressed vowel</u>. Then write each one in the correct <u>box</u>.

mis….rable   intellig….nce   mini….ture

parli….ment   desp….rate   deaf….ning   valu….ble

secret….ry

unstressed e

unstressed a

5

Complete the sentences below using words containing <u>unstressed vowels</u>.

I didn't recognise the word, so I looked it up in the d………………………… .

You don't have to go in fancy dress — it's v………………………… .

Noah had to read a lot for his degree in English l………………………… .

I hate pasta and sauce mixed together, so I keep them s………………………… .

6

Write each of these words in a <u>sentence</u>.

generous ⟶ …………………………………………………………

favourite ⟶ …………………………………………………………

animal ⟶ …………………………………………………………

Now Try This — Use the correct spelling of each word from question 2 in a sentence.

Homophones

Homophones are words that are **pronounced** the same, but have different **meanings** and **spellings**.

nose — Your nose is the part of your face used for breathing and smelling.

knows — To know something means to be aware of it.

1 Circle the correct word from each pair of homophones.

desert / dessert

heel / heal

mail / male

leek / leak

2 Fill in the gaps in the sentences below using the correct words from the box.

father / farther   heard / herd   guest / guessed

I had forgotten that we have a .... for dinner tonight.

Jasmine .... what was in the package by feeling it.

Lewis's .... is extremely strict.

The .... you go along the path, the higher it climbs.

One of the cows got separated from the rest of the ....

I .... my parents talking about my sister.

Section 15 — Confusing Words

3 Fill in the homophones in the boxes below. Then find all the words in the wordsearch.

night → | k | n | i | g | h | t |

bawl → | b | | | |

beech → | b | | | | |

daze → | d | | | |

blue → | b | | | |

pane → | p | | | |

steel → | s | | | | |

```
B A W L L B A E P
E D T H G I N B A
E   K E T B A L L N
C   N S T E A L E E
H   I B O A A P W N
T   G E L E E T S T
E   H A U G R O A P
U   T C F U H S T A
L R H U D A Z E I
B D A Y S C O U N
```

4 Draw a circle around the word that has been spelt incorrectly in each sentence. Write the correct spelling on the dotted line

I'm going on a cookery coarse in half term. ....

Led is a very heavy metal. ....

Please will you lone me this book? ....

I did worn you that this might happen. ....

5 Write each of these words in a sentence.

stationary → ....

stationery → ....

precede → ....

proceed → ....

Now Try This Think of a pair of homophones and write a sentence that uses both of them.

Section 15 — Confusing Words

Section 16 — Mixed Spelling Practice

Mixed Spelling Practice

1 Complete the words below using either ei or ie.

ach........ve   rec........pt   retr........ve   hyg........ne

misch........f   cash........r   perc........ve   shr........k

2 Put a tick in the boxes next to the words that are spelt correctly.
Put a cross in the boxes next to the words that are spelt incorrectly.

independent ☐   horrable ☐   emergency ☐

rodant ☐   miserible ☐   currancy ☐

referance ☐   intelligence ☐   impossible ☐

Write the correct spellings of the words you put a cross next to in the box below.

☐

3 Draw lines to match each word with the sound of its word ending.

technician   'shul'   operation

influential   spacious

special   'shun'   fiction

television   anxious

gracious   'shus'   partial

ambitious   artificial

4 Draw a circle around the word that has been spelt incorrectly in each sentence. Then write the correct spelling on the dotted line.

I recieved three bills in the post this morning. .... (received)

I am in no dougt that this is Katie's hairbrush. .... (doubt)

I'm having pancakes for breakfast this mourning. .... (morning)

That is not relevent to this conversation. .... (relevant)

We walked along the key at sunset. .... (quay)

5 Sort the words below into the correct group.

tough   sought   rough   thought

although   nought   though

dough   enough

'uff' sound

'oh' sound

'or' sound

6 Complete each sentence by adding a suffix to the root word in brackets.

Bushra did a lot of sport to keep .... (act).

She was the most .... (grace) dancer on the stage.

This is too complicated — we need to .... (simple) it.

The .... (electric) fixed the plug sockets after the power cut.

I'm studying biology but I would like to .... (special) in plants.

Section 16 — Mixed Spelling Practice

7 The answer to each of the clues below uses a <u>prefix</u> and a <u>root word</u> from each box. Solve the clues and <u>write</u> your answers in the boxes. Reading down the pink boxes will reveal a <u>hidden</u> message.

Prefixes: fore- under- mid- over- en- pre- em- non-

Root Words: wear large load sense day view bolden name

1. e.g. pants and socks
2. a sneak peek
3. make bigger
4. to load too heavily
5. noon
6. to make something bold
7. e.g. Jane or Owain
8. something that doesn't make sense

Hidden Message ➡ ....

8 Write a <u>homophone</u> for each of the words below. Then write a <u>sentence</u> which contains the new word you've written.

Look back at page 94 if you can't remember what homophones are.

billed ➡ ....

....

reign ➡ ....

....

peek ➡ ....

....

Glossary

Adjective — A word that describes a noun, e.g. **tricky** word, **angry** girl.

Adverb — A word that describes a **verb**, an **adjective** or other **adverbs**, e.g. **slowly**, **definitely**, **later**.

Adverbial — A group of words that behaves like an **adverb**.

Clause — Part of a sentence that contains a **subject** and a **verb**.

Conjunction — A word or phrase that **joins** two parts of a sentence, e.g. I play football and I play tennis.

Determiner — Tells you whether a **noun** is **general** or **specific**, e.g. She wants a car. She wants that car.

Exclamation — A sentence that shows **strong emotion**, beginning with 'how' or 'what'.

Fronted adverbial — An adverbial that comes at the **start** of a sentence.

Main clause — A clause that **makes sense** on its own, e.g. I sing in the shower while I wash my hair.

Modal verb — Can show how **likely** something is, e.g. We could go out.

Noun — A word that **names** something, e.g. **tiger**, **Michelle**, **Thursday**.

Preposition — Introduces a **pronoun**, **noun** or **noun phrase** and tells you **where**, **when** or **why** something happens, e.g. I am in front of the gate.

Pronoun — A word used to **replace** a **noun**, e.g. **I**, **we**, **they**.

Glossary

Relative clause — A **subordinate clause** that tells you more about a noun. It is often introduced by a **relative pronoun**, e.g. He's the man <u>who lives here</u>.

Subordinate clause — A clause that **doesn't make sense** on its own, e.g. I sing in the shower <u>while I wash my hair</u>.

Verb — A doing or being word, e.g. **walk**, **show**, **take**, **is**.

COMMON PUNCTUATION MARKS

Apostrophes — show **missing letters** and **possession**. | '

Brackets — **separate extra information** in a sentence. They can also be called '**parentheses**'. | ( )

Capital letters — used for **starting** sentences and for **names** or **I**. | A

Commas — used in **lists**, to **join clauses**, to separate **extra information** and after some **introductions**. | ,

Dashes — separate **extra information** in a sentence. | –

Exclamation marks — show **strong emotions** or **commands**. | !

Full stops — show where **sentences end**. | .

Inverted commas — show **direct speech**. | " "

Question marks — used at the **end** of **questions**. | ?

Answers

Grammar

Section 1 – Word Types

Page 4 – Nouns

1. Concrete nouns: **house**, **fish**, **grass**, **ball**, **bike**
   Abstract nouns: **faith**, **freedom**, **hope**, **anger**
   Collective nouns: **shoal**, **swarm**, **flock**, **herd**
2. Any suitable nouns. Examples:
   To get to the **butcher's**, I pass a field with a **flock** of **sheep**.
   The **excitement** I feel about going to **Birmingham** on the **train** is overwhelming.

Page 5 – Verbs

1. Drew **agrees** with his brother.
   We **are** going to **see** some friends tomorrow.
   He always **screams** when he sees a moth.
   Ikenna often **does** his homework straight after school.
2. **I am** captain of the county football team.
   I usually **dry my** wet hair with a towel.
   I go to night school twice a week.
   I have a new sports car.

Pages 6 and 7 – Modal Verbs

1. I **wouldn't** want to be famous.
   Aiden **should** change his socks.
   Sitara **may** know the answer.
   She **will** give us some advice.
   Yufei **should** know better.
   We **shall** do our very best.
   I **could** drive us there.
   Sally **might** move to Canada.
   They **can** come too.
2. Our holiday **should** have been relaxing, but it was very stressful.
   I **could** have gone with Finlay, but I had other things to do.
   That **might** be the answer, but I'm not so sure.
   Ken and Peter are away next week — they **must** let Chika know.
   The builders knew they **could** finish the job on time.
   I'm really not sure about what to do — I **might** ask a friend.
   Priti's not feeling well — she **should** stay in bed.
3. I **might** as well go to the party on my own.
   Norman would go on holiday to Australia if he **could** afford it.
   Would you like a piece of apple crumble?
   If you change your mind, you **should** let me know.
4. Any suitable answers.
   Examples:
   I might go to watch a football match tomorrow.
   I must go to see the head teacher.
   I will eat all of this pudding.
   I should buy my brother a birthday present.
   I shall be eleven next year.

Page 8 – Adjectives

1. You should have underlined: **aggressive**, **odd**, **rare**, **purple**, **cheeky**, **trendy**, **dismal**, **unusual**, **crazy**.
2. Any suitable adjectives.
   Examples:
   The play was **interesting** and the actors were **fabulous**.
   I had a **great** time.
   The concert was **awful** — the music was **terrible** and the food was **disgusting**.
3. Any suitable adjectives.
   Examples:
   There was a **strange** noise coming from the kitchen.
   The **enormous** monster in the cave is very angry.
   The **mischievous** monkeys will break our windscreen wipers.

Pages 9 to 11 – Adverbs

1. She played well. — **Verb**
   The party was bitterly disappointing. — **Adjective**
   The car is incredibly dirty. — **Adjective**
   Louise cheerfully waved to us. — **Verb**
   Sam seems extremely pleased. — **Adjective**
2. Tamina **accidentally** broke her mum's favourite vase.
   Olivia said she didn't feel **very** well.
   That house is **severely** damaged.
   The swans swam **elegantly** across the lake.
   The schoolboy **truthfully** answered the teacher's questions.
3. Certain: **definitely, surely, certainly**
   Not certain: **maybe, perhaps, possibly**
4. Any suitable sentences with a less certain adverb.
   Examples:
   It's **possibly** true that the weather wasn't good enough.
   Setting a deadline will **maybe** make a difference.
   My car will **perhaps** break down on the way.
5. Any suitable sentences with a more certain adverb.
   Examples:
   We will **definitely** go to see Grandma tomorrow.
   Francis and Gillian are **certainly** going to the cinema tonight.
   Surely Ulvertown Rovers will win the league.
6. Any suitable sentences.
   Examples:
   Perhaps the sun will come out this afternoon.
   Surely Jessica will be pleased with her results.
   Maybe the play will be a success.
   Karen is definitely the best player at our club.

Page 12 – Pronouns

1. Charlotte made a picture for Trudy, then gave **it** to **her**.
   Ed and Saira lost Zac, so **they** went to look for **him**.
2. I was cross with Dennis — **he** took my favourite top and tore **it**. He was sorry and said he would buy **me** a new one. My sister was angry with **him** too — he borrowed her scissors and broke **them**. But never mind, **we** are all friends again now.

Answers

Answers

Page 13 – Relative Pronouns

1. We met the acrobat .... performed in the circus. — **who**
   I like the blue shoes .... have sparkly laces. — **which**
   They always stay in hotels .... have a five-star rating. — **which**
   Joel is the builder .... built our house. — **who**
   Lauren saw the dentist .... gave her a filling. — **who**

2. We have a new neighbour **who** works at the bank.
   This is the shop **which/that** sells diving equipment.
   Geraldine owns a house **which/that** has four bedrooms.
   That's the woman **whose** daughter is a famous footballer.

Page 14 – Determiners

1. **The** teacher told us **a** funny story about **an** elephant in **the** jungle.
   We saw **a** picture of **that** house by **the** river where **your** boat is.
   Ben and Euan finally changed **those** light bulbs in **their** bathroom.
   A police officer chased **some** thieves out of **the** bank and into **an** alleyway.

2. Any suitable determiners.
   Examples:
   That pizza is the best pizza I've ever tasted.
   We need to go to the garage — **our** car has broken down.
   Add **some** milk — any amount is fine.
   Kelly saw **an** aardvark and **a** lion at the zoo.

Section 2 – Clauses and Phrases

Page 15 – Clauses

1. You should have ticked:
   <u>Darius went to the shop</u> because he needed some milk.
   Unless you know the answer, <u>we'll ask Zeynep</u>.
   <u>They climbed the tree</u> even though I thought it was a bad idea.

2. Any suitable clauses.
   Examples:
   We need to wait **until we're allowed to go in**.
   Eleanor has a shower **after going to the gym**.
   I'm going to buy some sweets **when we get to the shop**.
   Doris wants to get a dog **although her parents say she can't**.
   Abeba eats her breakfast **before going to school**.

Pages 16 and 17 – Basic Relative Clauses

1. You should have circled the words in bold and underlined these clauses:
   I prefer the blue shoes **which** <u>match my dress</u>.
   This is the house **that** <u>Megan is going to move into</u>.
   I don't like people **who** <u>are cruel to animals</u>.
   We found a lost dog **whose** <u>owner was nowhere to be seen</u>.
   Yvonne likes to go for walks **that** <u>have amazing views</u>.
   This is the computer game **that** <u>I bought last weekend</u>.

2. This is the book **which/that** Pria was reading.
   The Tasty Taverna is a restaurant **which/that** specialises in vegetarian meals.
   I need to find a shop **which/that** sells fancy dress costumes.
   Ulrika met a man **whose** dog was almost as big as he was.
   Juliet is the person **who/that** always gets her own way.
   Let's go on holiday to a country **which/that** has hot, sunny weather.
   We saw a jellyfish **whose** tentacles were two metres long.

3. I found an injured rabbit whose leg was broken.
   Scott moved to a quiet village where there were no other children.
   Mum is looking for a builder who can renovate our house.
   Themba remembers the day when he got lost at the funfair.
   Colin wants to buy the game that he saw advertised on TV.

4. Any suitable relative clauses.
   Examples:
   Susanna waited for Edward, **who was stuck in traffic**.
   There was a lot of noise, **which was very distracting**.
   Ronald went to the circus, **which had acrobats**.
   The people welcomed the man **who had a parrot on his shoulder**.

5. Any suitable sentences.
   Examples:
   The teacher, **who was very busy**, gave the class extra homework.
   The scientist made an everlasting cake, **which was his best experiment so far**.

Pages 18 and 19 – Trickier Relative Clauses

1. Hibo, **who wants to be a pilot**, is taking flying lessons.
   After the party, **which finished at midnight**, we went to bed.
   The room **where the books are stored** is being repainted.
   That day **when I fell over** was the most embarrassing day of my life.
   The house **that flooded during the storm** can now be lived in again.
   Eugeniusz, **whose son plays the drums in a band**, loves rock music.

2. Any suitable relative clauses.
   Examples:
   The boy **whose paper aeroplane had crashed** looked very angry.
   Michael's phone, **which cost a lot of money**, broke.
   The town **where Melissa is moving to** is not very big.
   Roger's nephew, **who plays the piano**, is twelve.
   That windy day **when our tent blew away** was awful.
   My old teddy bear, **which I've had for ten years**, is in the wash.

3. You should have ticked:
   The museum which we visited was very interesting.
   That's the football team that Josh is joining.
   My tenth birthday was the day that I was chased by a squirrel.

4. The walk we went on was far too long.
   I've forgotten the name of the film Jim recommended.
   She can't remember the day we went to the zoo.

Answers

Page 20 – Phrases

1. Phrase: **behind the blue sofa**, **on the phone**, **little pork sausages**, **at the back**, **those naughty boys**, **long, hairy legs**.
   Clause: **he's silly**, **Ray sat down**, **we're happy**, **let's play golf**, **I go swimming**, **they're fine**.
2. Riku lost <u>his red, fluffy mittens</u>.
   <u>The man in the waterproof coat</u> ate a sandwich.
   <u>One type of penguin</u> lives in South Africa.
   Willow read <u>a long book about a yam called Gavin</u>.
   The big dog ran after <u>the bouncing yellow tennis ball</u>.
   <u>A tired explorer with a big backpack</u> walked over the wide mountain range.

Section 3 – Conjunctions and Prepositions

Page 21 – Co-ordinating Conjunctions

1. I'd like to go to Australia, **but** it's too expensive.
   In the cellar it was dark, **and** there were lots of strange noises.
   Please give this letter to a parent, **or** give it to a guardian.
   Playing near busy roads is dangerous, **so** you shouldn't do it.
   Mabel felt completely relaxed, **for** she was on holiday.
2. I would like a drink **and** I would like some food.
   Fran's remark was hurtful, **but** it was also true.
   My pencil was blunt **so** I used a pen.

Page 22 – Subordinating Conjunctions

1. Help yourself to a glass of water <u>if</u> you are thirsty.
   <u>Unless</u> your dad says you can't, you can come to the cinema.
   <u>Although</u> it might sound silly, I quite like going for walks in the rain.
   Marian goes to see her uncle in hospital <u>when</u> she is not busy.
   Fletcher watches TV programmes <u>while</u> he eats his lunch.
2. I have lived here **since** I was five.
   I follow my brother **wherever** he goes.
   My sister always smiles **while** she is dancing.
   I like Pierre **even though** he can be a bit annoying.
   The dog can't come in **because** his paws are dirty.

Page 23 – Using Conjunctions for Cohesion

1. Any suitable conjunctions used to join the sentences.
   Examples:
   I was going to miss the train, **so** I began to run.
   We might go shopping **or** we might go cycling.
2. Any suitable conjunctions used to make the passage flow better.
   Examples:
   School was closed today **because** the heating was broken. The pupils went home, **but** no one complained. They went to the park **while** the teachers stayed at school.

Pages 24 and 25 – Prepositions

1. Any sentences using sensible prepositions.
   Examples:
   There are flowers **under the window**.
   There is a bird **on the roof**.
   There is a tree **next to the house**.
   There are bushes **around the house**.
   There is a path **in front of the house**.
2. You should have circled these words:
   That picture **on** the wall is absolutely horrible.
   I ate lots of popcorn **during** the film.
   Iris has been playing the guitar **since** 10 pm.
   Jamila is meeting her dad **in front of** the supermarket.
   We can't do anything **until** the day after tomorrow.
   Let's put up posters **in** any available space.
   They buried the time capsule **underneath** the oak tree.
3. **On** Friday, I'm going to the dentist.
   I think there's a mistake **in** my work.
   The woman in the cinema told us to stop talking **during** the film.
   Our school is open **from** 8 am **until** 4 pm.
   The shop isn't open, so people are forming a queue **outside** the door.
   I always listen to music **after** dinner.
4. Any sentence that uses at least two prepositions correctly.
   Examples:
   I waited **outside** the cinema patiently **until** 9 pm.
5. Any sentences that use prepositions correctly.
   Examples:
   My bed is **in the middle of** the room. **Next to** the bed I have a small table, and **on** the table there is a lamp and a clock. My wardrobe is **at the end of** the room, **beside** the window. I have three posters **on** the walls.

Section 4 – Linking Ideas

Pages 26 and 27 – Linking Ideas in a Paragraph

1. You should have circled these phrases:
   over there
   after a while
   twice a year
   every time
   the other day
   near the wall
   very slowly
2. The chest was unlocked. <u>Without a sound</u>, Susie opened the lid.
   It's a hot day. You should put suncream on <u>after lunch</u>.
   I do after-school activities <u>four times a week</u>. It's exhausting but fun.
   There are one hundred tadpoles <u>in the school pond</u>. We're studying them.
   The bus arrived. Thomas ate his breakfast <u>ridiculously fast</u>.
   There was so much to do. Tina didn't stop painting <u>until midnight</u>.
   My bedroom was a mess. I hid all the toys and books <u>under the bed</u>.

Answers

3. Yesterday, I went to an amazing activity day. <u>First</u> we had to register, and then we played some warm-up games. <u>At 10 am</u>, we raced each other through a great obstacle course. We ate <u>in the garden</u>, and <u>after lunch</u> we built a big tree house. <u>Finally</u> we made rafts and raced them <u>in two separate teams</u>.
4. Example sentences:
   I am making a kite. After tea, I will try it out.
   The witch looked around. She crept up the stairs very quietly.
   It is Christmas Eve. Tomorrow morning, it will be Christmas Day.

Pages 28 and 29 – Linking Paragraphs

1. You should have matched these pairs:
   <u>Later</u>, the nurse looked at my ankle. She said it was broken in two places. — time
   <u>Thirdly</u>, I started to screw the different pieces together, one at a time. — number
   <u>At Grandad's house</u>, Clare set up the chessboard and made two cups of tea. — place
2. You should have drawn lines to match these words and phrases:
   Place: in Ian's room, next to him, at the garage, above that, behind me
   Number: secondly, thirdly, fourthly, firstly
   Time: this week, at 5 pm, before breakfast, every day
3. In the morning, George went to buy the ingredients for his lemon cake. It took over an hour.
   <u>That afternoon</u>, he started mixing and measuring.

   Secondly, I covered the exercise book in colourful patterned paper.
   <u>Thirdly</u>, I used some sticky plastic to make the book waterproof and keep it looking neat.

   My brother Jeremy loves doing science experiments — even in the house!
   <u>Last week</u>, he mixed lots of Mum's hair products together. It exploded everywhere!

   I was really enjoying the spaghetti Dad had made for tea, but I kept dropping bits accidentally.
   <u>Under the table</u>, our cat was eating the scraps, but he couldn't manage the spaghetti!
4. My uncle always **bakes** me a special cake. Last year, he **came** to my party with a giant sprout. I **was** horrified! But when he cut it open, it wasn't a sprout at all! He **had made** a chocolate cake that looked like a sprout. This year's cake **looks** even more extraordinary.

Section 5 – Verb Tenses

Page 30 – Present Tense and Past Tense

1. <u>pack</u> — We packed the car.
   <u>pay</u> — I paid the bills.
   <u>throw</u> — They threw it out.
   <u>paints</u> — He painted a picture.
   <u>does</u> — Yaling did a lot.
2. Any sentences about the pictures which are in the correct tense.
   Examples:
   Present: The villain sneaks around.
   Past: The robber crept away from the police.
   Present: The man holds the spanner.
   Past: The mechanic fixed the car.

Page 31 – Verbs with 'ing'

1. We were starting, but they were finishing.
   Mark and Niamh were skiing, but I was freezing!
   I was running, she was jogging and they were sitting.
2. My brother Micah is **leaving** home today. Six months ago he was **applying** to boarding school, and he was **hoping** to get a place. Now he's actually **going**. I will miss him because he's always **helping** me with my homework. I am already **counting** down the days until half term.

Page 32 – The Present Perfect

1. Khadija has decided not to move house.
   Martha has been to the shops.
   Ralph has taken Lilly's toys.
2. I have planned a surprise for Ann because she has passed her exams. I have chosen a really good film at the cinema, and I have booked tickets for us.

Section 6 – Standard and Non-Standard English

Pages 33 to 35 – Standard and Non-Standard English

1. She were an amazing player. — N
   I am going fishing today. — S
   Last week, I run five miles. — N
   Have you finished your dinner? — S
   You are very tall, Mr Grew. — S
   I will played sport later. — N
   That are an awful story. — N
   We are listening to music. — S
   I eat two muffins yesterday. — N
   I am building a spaceship. — S

Answers

2. You should have crossed out these words:
   Kevin must (have / ~~of~~) (gone / ~~went~~) on another special mission.
   I would (have / ~~of~~) asked Stuart, but he (~~gone~~ / went) home.
   You should (have / ~~of~~) asked before you (~~done~~ / did) it without me.
   I (saw / ~~seen~~) my grandparents earlier when they (came / ~~come~~) over.
   Abdul (~~come~~ / came) downstairs because he had (done / ~~did~~) his homework.
   We might (have / ~~of~~) left the pencils where we (~~done~~ / did) the drawing.

3. Go and ask **those** people if they'll help us carry it.
   I was so hungry that I ate **them** all in one go.
   Take **those** photos over to the windowsill, please.
   I saw **them** steal the stickers at lunchtime.
   Nicola and **I** both play the trombone.
   My cousin is teaching **me** to do karate.
   It's my turn because they found **me** first.
   Oli and **I** are planning a surprise party.

4. You should have circled and corrected these words:
   It **are** just down... — is
   I **is** helping them... — am
   Dad **say** the decorating... — says
   now we **is** getting... — are
   Dad **bake** all the bread... — bakes
   Mum **do** everything else... — does
   lots of people **visits**... — visit

5. I haven't got nothing. — 2
   My dad hasn't got a beard. — 1
   We don't have no biscuits left. — 2
   Connor won't go nowhere. — 2
   I can't tell you the secret. — 1
   They haven't got a sister. — 1
   David doesn't like broccoli. — 1
   You can't see nothing in here. — 2
   No one said nothing to me. — 2
   We mustn't do anything yet. — 1
   Oliver couldn't find anyone. — 1
   Ha-Yun wasn't helping no one. — 2

6. Any suitable sentences that use the correct grammar.
   Examples:
   I am not very well.
   We are not sure.
   Raj is not going.
   Chloe has not got it.
   I am not finished. / I have not finished.
   He is not here.

Punctuation

Section 7 – Sentence Punctuation

Page 36 – Capital Letters and Full Stops

1. You should have circled: eiffel tower, spain, ashley, friday, christmas
2. You should have ticked:
   My step-mum's favourite sweets can only be bought in Canada.
   Ellis's dog is called Spot. Spot is a Dalmatian.
   I play cricket every Friday evening.
   Corrected sentences:
   Mrs Flint is thirty-two. **H**er birthday is in **M**ay.
   My **b**est **f**riend is called Amy. She lives in Bath**.**

Page 37 – Question Marks

1. Where are you going on holiday**?**
   Here are those gloves you lost**.**
   Let's go shopping tomorrow**.**
   Is this your idea of a joke**?**
   Would you like ketchup**?**
   Are you feeling OK, Kinga**?**
   I don't know how to fry an egg**.**
   What's happening out there**?**
   It's raining a lot this week**.**
   We should order pizzas**.**
2. Any sensible question that begins with a capital letter and ends with a question mark.
   Examples:
   Who would like to take the map?
   What shall I bring with me?
   Would you like some chicken?
   Can you pick me up from Annie's later?

Page 38 – Exclamation Marks

1. You should have ticked:
   Shut up
   Stop that, now
   Quick, get out of here
2. Ouch, that really hurt**!**
   My brother is really good at playing the piano**.**
   Watch out, it's going to fall over**!**
   The bathroom is the second door on the left**.**
3. Any sentences that show strong emotion or something that would be said loudly and end with an exclamation mark.
   Examples:
   Thanks for inviting me to this wonderful party**!**
   I've had an absolutely terrible day**!**

Page 39 – Sentence Practice

1. Jon asked when they were leaving**.** **(statement)**
   How ridiculous those shoes are**!** **(exclamation)**
   Switch the appliance off at the mains**.** **(command)**
   What time do you think we should leave**?** **(question)**
   What an incredible cake that is**!** **(exclamation)**

Answers

2. Any suitable sentences that use capital letters and punctuation correctly.
   Example:
   Harriet is on holiday, and she wants to go sightseeing.
   Are you ready to be chopped up, little vegetables**?**
   Oh no — my racket is broken and I don't have a spare one**!**

Section 8 – Commas

Pages 40 and 41 – Commas in Lists

1. I am going to the supermarket with my mum, her sister and my best friend. We need to buy some more cereal, a couple of pints of milk, a pack of dishcloths and some baking ingredients. We are going to bake some chocolate-chip cookies, a batch of flapjacks, a sponge cake and a raspberry cheesecake. We haven't got any flour, butter, sugar or raspberries at the moment.

2. You will need 500 g sugar, 200 g flour, 300 g butter and some raisins.
   Please bring a packed lunch, a swimming costume and a few pens.
   The journey was quite long, very tiring and really boring.

3. I need to clean the kitchen, bake some flapjacks, do my homework and tidy my bedroom.

4. Enter the competition to win a microwave, a brand-new camera, a week's supply of cake **or** (OR **and**) two theatre tickets.
   On the walk we saw a herd of cows, lots of benches, a squirrel **and** two rabbits.

Pages 42 and 43 – Commas to Avoid Confusion

1. No, babies are cute.
   I don't want to fight, Jade.
   Clara loves painting, books and baking cakes.
   I only told my parents, James, and Aneesah.

2. Any suitable explanation. Example:
   Without a comma, the sentence means I'm frightened of two things: cricket bats (the sports equipment) and thunderstorms.
   With a comma, the sentence means I'm frightened of three things: cricket (the sport), bats (the animal) and thunderstorms.

3. Any drawings that show two items on the table in the first picture (chocolate-flavoured cake and crisps) and three items on the table in the second picture (chocolate, cake and crisps).

4. As the man turned blue, doctors started to worry.
   Ella's favourite things are summer, holidays and going on long walks.
   It's time to start cooking, children.
   I took a photo of the woman, with a camera.
   Max, the neighbour's cat, is making strange noises.

Pages 44 and 45 – Commas After Subordinate Clauses

1. As I got on the bus, I dropped my bag.
   Although I am scared of sharks, I love visiting the aquarium.
   Once I'd finished eating, I started reading my new book.
   Rather than going out, we stayed in and watched a film.

2. <u>While you were distracted</u>, I swapped our plates.
   You can go to the party <u>as long as you wear something sensible</u>.
   <u>Now that you've told me that</u>, everything makes much more sense.
   <u>Until we've found the solution</u>, we'll keep trying to work it out.
   I'll come and help you <u>as soon as I can</u>.
   <u>Since we're all here</u>, I'd like to tell you something.

3. The sentences that need commas are:
   When I realised what I'd done, I apologised immediately.
   Although I like the album, this song isn't my favourite.
   As you're older than me, you should go first.

4. Even though it was cold, I wanted ice cream.
   Despite the fact we lost, we still had fun.
   Whereas Steffen is calm, Nima is always stressed.
   Before I left the house, I turned the lights off.

5. Any correct subordinate clause that ends with a comma.
   Examples:
   After I've eaten, I need to ring my sister.
   Despite Ollie's rude comments, Raf wasn't offended.
   Even though the film was very frightening, Karthik wasn't scared.

Pages 46 and 47 – Commas After Fronted Adverbials

1. As quietly as possible, Adil crept downstairs.
   Very quickly, Ebele jumped out of bed.
   In ten years' time, my parents will be sixty.
   Earlier today, my teacher gave me detention.
   In a very silly way, Ciaran skipped across the yard.
   In the kitchen, there's a present for you.

2. You should have ticked:
   Before dawn, everything is very peaceful.
   As quickly as possible, he packed his bags.
   Under the new rules, we can't wear jewellery to school.
   Corrected sentences:
   In Italy, pizza and pasta are very popular foods.
   Last week, the boys won the football match.

3. Before school, Kim made her packed lunch.
   On Tuesday, I am going to the cinema.
   Every morning, my mum runs 5 km.
   In town, there is a really big skate park.

4. On the left, you can see my old house.
   Every year, we visit my aunt.
   Like a mouse, she crept through the house.
   Earlier than usual, she set off for school.

Answers

Pages 48 and 49 – Commas for Extra Information

1. You should have ticked:
   The flight, even though it felt really long, only took three hours.
   Dr Grey, our family doctor, told me to try to get more sleep.
   Corrected sentences:
   My brothers, who are twins, are called Eamon and Archie.
   We saw my teacher, Mr Harris, in the park.

2. On Thursday, the day after tomorrow, I am going on holiday. I am going with my two sisters, Izzy and Amelia, and our mum. We're spending a few days in Portugal, a really hot country, before flying back to England. The holiday, which was quite expensive, should be really fun.

3. The charity auction, which raised hundreds of pounds, was a great success.
   Pepperoni, my favourite pizza topping, is a kind of sausage.
   The shepherd, who'd lost all his sheep, was very upset.

4. Charles Dickens, a famous English writer, was born in 1812.
   My pet mice, called Sammy and Sally, are adorable.
   My parents, who met fifteen years ago, get on really well.

Pages 50 and 51 – Comma Practice

1. You should have ticked:
   The Alps, a European mountain range, are popular with skiers.
   At the beach, I had an ice cream and read my book.
   My favourite fruits are apples, oranges, pears and strawberries.
   Mrs Williams, our window cleaner, fell off her ladder yesterday.
   Corrected sentences:
   The bus stops on King Street, Russel Lane and Victoria Square.
   The book, about electricity, looks quite difficult.
   In England, the weather is often grey and cloudy.
   Even if I knew it, I wouldn't tell you the answer.

2. Many people came to the fair <u>until it started to rain</u>.
   <u>While she was shopping</u>, we prepared her surprise.
   <u>Even though I love most fruits</u>, I hate apples.
   <u>If I get home in time</u>, I'll start making our tea.
   <u>Although the pirate was very scary</u>, her parrot was hilarious.
   You can help me with the decorations <u>since you're so early</u>.
   <u>Provided that you've brought your trunks</u>, we can go swimming today.
   You can't go to football practice <u>unless you've done your homework</u>.

3. Any suitable explanations. Examples:
   The first sentence means that people were looking at the shops in a town square, but the second sentence means that square-shaped people were looking at the shops in a town.
   Adding a comma changes the sentence from a list of two things (history teachers and detention) to a list of three things (history, teachers and detention).

Section 9 – Brackets and Dashes

Pages 52 and 53 – Brackets for Extra Information

1. You should have ticked:
   Rhinos (an endangered species) mostly live in Africa.
   Umaru was late to work yesterday (Tuesday).
   The competition was won by Mr Fairclough (a train driver).
   Our neighbour (Mrs Bewley) forgot to put the bins out.

2. Our friends (James (and Alun) live across the road.
   (When we went fishing (last weekend), I caught nothing.
   It was too hot (thirty-six degrees) for the cat) to go outside.
   The majority of us (seventy-five) per cent) wanted Fraser to win.
   Agata and Akhil (our (aunt and uncle) gave us a new sofa.

3. The portrait (painted in 1839) cost Mr Dough a lot of money.
   Fatima finished her knitting (a woolly jumper).
   There are eleven players (including a goalkeeper) in a hockey team.
   Logan's tie (black with sparkly bits) had a hole in it.

4. Jenny and Barbara (the identical twins) work at the same shop.
   Arthur Coddle (an English author) wrote several novels.
   The café is closed on Mondays (the manager's day off).
   'The Rising Sea' (my favourite book) is about mermaids.
   The poodle (a breed of dog) has lots of fur.

5. Any suitable phrases. Examples:
   The main course (roast beef) was delicious.
   Hazel's dog (a Cocker Spaniel) likes to chase tennis balls.
   The workers (who were on strike) didn't turn up for work.
   Indira's favourite toy (a rag doll) was very old.
   Rodney's car (a yellow three-wheeler) pulled up outside.
   The supermarket (the one at the end of the street) is overrun by mice.

Pages 54 and 55 – Dashes for Extra Information

1. You should have crossed this sentence:
   We built — a sandcastle a big one — on the beach.
   The correct sentence is:
   We built a sandcastle — a big one — on the beach.

2. Mr Miller — the county's finest baker — has announced his plans to bake Britain's first gingerbread hotel. The hotel — four storeys high — will open next summer. Six thousand people — many from the local area — have applied to stay at the hotel during the first month. Mr Miller's son — also a baker — will be in charge of the construction of the hotel. Two tonnes of ginger — grown specially by Mr Miller — will be used in the project. Tim Bury — a famous architect — thinks that the plan will simply not work.

3. Moussa and Sonny — the carpenters — need some new tools.
   There is a box of chocolates — a big box — in the kitchen.
   Adam forgot his lunch — yet again — this morning.
   Hayley — a famous comedian — is performing tonight.

4. My cat — a tabby — likes to eat tuna.
   Lea's mum — a talented singer — is in the opera.
   The waltzer — a type of ride — makes me dizzy.

Answers

Section 10 – Apostrophes

Page 56 – Apostrophes for Missing Letters

1. she will — she'll
   they have — they've
   who would — who'd
   he is — he's
   they are — they're
   where is — where's
   that will — that'll
   must not — mustn't

2. Any sentence containing the shortened version of each pair of words, with an apostrophe in the correct place.
   Examples:
   I should've left home earlier this morning.
   It might've happened already.
   She won't tell anyone your secret.
   You could've walked to my house.

Page 57 – Apostrophes for Single Possession

1. puppy's
   bus's
   Jess's
   kite's
   pot's

2. You should have added an apostrophe and an 's' to these words:
   Ellenby's
   Rosie's
   Ahmed's
   band's
   Robin's

3. Any two sentences which use an apostrophe and an 's' to show possession correctly.
   Examples:
   The woman's nails are blue.
   The cowboy's trousers are red.

Page 58 – Apostrophes for Plural Possession

1. You should have crossed out these phrases:
   the sisters's
   the womens'
   the birds's
   the mices'

2. The students' books are heavy.
   The dice's spots are black.
   The guitars' strings are metal.
   The children's bricks are blue.
   The owls' eyes are big.

Page 59 – Its and It's

1. You should have ticked:
   It's fun to travel abroad.
   It's taken no time at all.
   It's my birthday today.
   The lion chased its prey.
   The baby threw its toys.
   Corrected sentences:
   It's got to work this time.
   The panda ate its dinner.
   It's time to go home now.

2. **It's** not dark outside yet.
   Its stripes are black and white.
   Its park has a jungle gym.
   It's important to eat fruit.
   Its sign is falling down.
   It's the busiest shop in town.
   Its home is under the floor.
   It's got to be finished later.

Pages 60 and 61 – Apostrophe Practice

1. what will — what'll
   are not — aren't
   you would — you'd
   who is — who's
   when has — when's
   does not — doesn't

2.
is not	isn't	let us	let's
where will	where'll	has not	hasn't
why is	why's	we would	we'd
have not	haven't	he is (OR) he has	he's
might have	might've	should not	shouldn't

3. You should have added these apostrophes:
   My **hamster's** name is Hector, and **I've** had him for two years.
   The shark showed its teeth and swam towards the **fisherman's** boat.
   It's been a great day, but now the park is shutting its gates.
   Dina's going to her **dad's** house tomorrow because **it's** Wednesday.

4. The cars' old engines
   The women's red coats
   The dresses' thin straps
   The tigers' sharp claws
   The men's good work

5. You should have matched these pairs:
   the girl's cats — one girl owns two cats
   the girls' cats — two girls own two cats
   the girl's cat — one girl owns one cat
   the girls' cat — two girls own one cat

6. Any two sentences where one uses 'its' correctly and the other uses 'it's' correctly.
   Examples:
   The rabbit is eating its carrot.
   It's a rabbit eating a carrot.

Answers

Section 11 – Inverted Commas

Pages 62 and 63 – Punctuating Speech

1. Fred said happily, "This is going to be the best weekend ever."
    "Rachel, stop that at once!" shouted her aunt.
    "Please may I buy some sweets to take home?" asked Hannah.
    Arundhati said, "We need to take a packed lunch with us today."
    "I want to go and see the tigers first," said Anna excitedly.
2. "Are you going to the party"? asked Mirek. — punctuation mark in the wrong place
    Dad shouted, "dinner is ready!" — missing capital letter
    Emily said "I have a baby brother." — missing comma
    "I'm practising all the time", said Max. — punctuation mark in the wrong place
    "This cookie is delicious " said Sophie. — missing comma
    My sister asked, "is this your skirt?" — missing capital letter
    Nasreen shouted "Come here please!" — missing comma
3. The children shouted, "We love Grantham School Hockey Team!"
    "Today I am going to talk about my hobby," said Nicholas.
    "What are we going to do with this monkey?" asked Molly.
    "Have you got your passport and your ticket?" my aunt asked.
    Yasmin yelled, "I can see the theme park over there!"
    "Can we change the channel, please?" asked Yusif.
4. "I don't feel very well at all," said Harry.
    Shufen asked, "How do I get to the station?"
    "There's a fire in the gym!" yelled William.
5. Any sentence which uses inverted commas correctly with the words in the box. Example:
    "Did you score at football today?" Mum asked.

Page 64 – Punctuating Speech in Two Parts

1. You should have ticked these sentences:
    "At long last," said the villain, "the whole world will be mine!"
    "Excuse me," said the lady, "do you know what time it starts?"
2. "This drink," said Cerys, "tastes of nothing."
    "I think," said Rob, "it's just round here."
    "And then," said Sam, "he just disappeared!"
3. "I think," said Gwen, "that we should all go."
    "Just focus," said Nia, "and it will be fine."

Section 12 – Paragraphs and Layout

Pages 65 and 66 – Paragraphs

1. Any suitable sentences about the same subject.
    Examples:
    You can use them to play computer games.
    It was really scary at first but then I got used to it.

2. You should have added these paragraph markers:
    On Tuesday I was playing outside with my friend Mia. She is a great skateboarder. I don't have a skateboard of my own, so I asked Mia if I could have a go on hers. I really wanted to practise. // "No," said Mia, "you're not as good as me so you might break it." // Last year, Mia got eight chocolate eggs for Easter but she wouldn't let anyone else have any. I don't think Mia is very good at sharing.
    Correct reasons:
    2nd paragraph — new person speaks
    3rd paragraph — new time
3. You should have added these paragraph markers:
    "This is hopeless," moaned Ashling, "I can't do it." The maths exercise had taken her most of the lesson already. // "It's easy," said Jack. "You're forgetting to add the seven, that's all." // Ashling wasn't impressed. She covered the page with her arms and scowled at him. // "Don't worry, Jack" said Tracy. "Ashling never lets anyone help."
    You should have rewritten the passage like this:
    　"This is hopeless," moaned Ashling, "I can't do it." The maths exercise had taken her most of the lesson already.
    　"It's easy," said Jack. "You're forgetting to add the seven, that's all."
    　Ashling wasn't impressed. She covered the page with her arms and scowled at him.
    　"Don't worry, Jack," said Tracy. "Ashling never lets anyone help."

Page 67 – Headings and Subheadings

1. You should have matched these pairs:
    Welcome to Paradise — An advert for a luxury holiday
    A Treat for Your Taste Buds — A review of a local restaurant
    More Than Just Books — A leaflet promoting the library
2. Any three subheadings which match the content of the paragraphs.
    Examples:
    The Best Quality Teaching
    After-School Activities for All
    Top of the Range Technology

Answers

Spelling

Section 13 – Prefixes

Pages 68 and 69 – Prefixes – 'under', 'over', 'en' and 'em'

1. **over**slept, **over**grown, **under**staffed, **under**populated, **over**crowded, **under**qualified
2. **paid** — **over**paid, **under**paid
   value — **over**value, **under**value
3. **em**bolden, **en**courage, **en**act, **en**rage, **em**pathise, **em**power, **en**danger, **en**circle, **en**force
4. **en**large, **en**liven, **em**bitter, **en**close
5. Any sentence where the word is used correctly.
   Examples:
   Frank bought an **oversized** T-shirt.
   I think the new Shakespeare film is **underrated**.
   The kite string got **entangled** in the trees.

Pages 70 and 71 – Prefixes – 'mid', 'pre', 'fore' and 'non'

1. The **mid**term test will take place on Tuesday.
   If you would like to take part, you need to **pre**register.
   The problem with pollution is at the **fore**front of the agenda.
2. **pre**mature, **fore**head, **non**fiction, **fore**ground, **pre**date, **mid**way, **mid**summer, **mid**week, **pre**program
3. **fore**see, **pre**book, **mid**morning, **non**refillable, **mid**air, **fore**court
4. **fore**cast, **mid**fielder, **mid**section, **pre**school, **mid**day, **Mid**winter, **pre**selected, **pre**view
5. The jungle ball ends at **midnight** with fireworks.
   I can't understand my little brother — he speaks **nonsense**.
   Crocodiles look like **prehistoric** creatures.
   The workers received instructions from the **foreman**.
   The children were at the **midpoint** of the project.

Pages 72 and 73 – Hyphenating Prefixes

1. **re-examine, pro-American, co-ordinate, re-emerge, pre-order, co-exist**
2. **pre-own, re-elect, anti-American, re-enter, anti-ageing, pro-European, co-owner**
3. Samira **re-sent** her letter to the mayor after receiving no reply.
   Brad didn't **resent** the fact that Stu beat him in the 100 m hurdles.
   Many people are against the government's plans for **reform**.
   The synchronised swimmers **re-formed** to create a heart shape.
   Henry used invisible ink by mistake, so he had to **re-sign** the form.
   Julie had an argument with her boss and decided to **resign**.
   After mixing up the documents, we had to **re-sort** them.
   We had to **resort** to pushing our car to the garage.
4. I help my friends as much as possible — it's good to **co**-operate.
   Kasia and Rhys are **co**-authors of a best-selling novel.
   No one applied for the job, so the position will be **re**-advertised.
5. Any sentence where the word has been used correctly.
   Examples:
   Thank you very much for your **co-operation**.
   We learnt about the **anti-slavery** movement in our History lesson.

Section 14 – Word Endings and Suffixes

Pages 74 and 75 – Word Endings – The 'shun' Sound

1. You should have underlined: **mencian, hesitacian, attencian, beautition**.
   The correct spellings are: **mention, hesitation, attention, beautician**.
2. musi**cian**, invita**tion**, fric**tion**, mathemati**cian**, opti**cian**, comple**tion**
3. deci**sion**, colli**sion**, permi**ssion**, ten**sion**, conclu**sion**, intru**sion**
4. in**tention**, ma**gician**, dis**cussion**, op**eration**, el**ectrician**, so**lution**

Page 76 – Word Endings – The 'shus' Sound

1. overcau**tious**, suspi**cious**, cons**cious**, atro**cious**
2. You should have circled these words:
   delicious, precious, vicious, fictitious
   You should have filled in:
   fictitious, vicious, delicious, precious
3. Any sentence where the word is used correctly.
   Examples:
   Julian is very **ambitious**.
   I try to eat a **nutritious** meal every day.

Page 77 – Word Endings – The 'shul' Sound

1. spe**cial**, poten**tial**, ini**tial**, confiden**tial**
2. mar**tial**, essen**tial**, artifi**cial**, so**cial**, substan**tial**, influen**tial**
3. ra**cial**, par**tial**, spa**cial**

Pages 78 and 79 – Word Endings – 'ant' and 'ent'

1. You should have ticked: **independent** and **innocent**.
   You should have crossed: **arrogent, instrumant, hesitent** and **expectent**.
   The correct spellings are: **arrogant, instrument, hesitant** and **expectant**.
2. mom**ent**, relev**ant**, toler**ant**, perman**ent**, evid**ent**, dist**ant**, tal**ent**
3. You should have circled: **commant, vacent, independant, anciant**.
   The correct spellings are: **comment, vacant, independent, ancient**.
4. Across: 1. **elephant** 2. **comment**
   Down: 1. **accident** 2. **silent** 3. **absent** 4. **present**

Answers

Pages 80 and 81 — Word Endings — 'ance', 'ancy' and 'ence', 'ency'

1. **science**, **refer**ence, **pati**ence, **guid**ance, **bal**ance
2. **decency**, **resist**ance, **evid**ence, **influ**ence, **effici**ency, **urg**ency, **reli**ance
3. independ**ence**, intellig**ence**, subst**ance**, experi**ence**
4. **vacancy**, **emerg**ency, **frequ**ency, **pregn**ancy, **expect**ancy
5. **perform**ance, **curr**ency, **fragr**ance, **absorb**ency

Pages 82 and 83 — Word Endings — 'able', 'ible', 'ably' and 'ibly'

1. **reasonably**, **adjustable**, **flexible**, **incredibly**
2. considerable — **considerably**
   applicable — **applicably**
   horrible — **horribly**
   responsible — **responsibly**
   reliable — **reliably**
   comfortable — **comfortably**
   adorable — **adorably**
3. accept**able**, change**able**, ined**ible**, sens**ibly**, question**able**, terr**ibly**, understand**ably**, miser**ably**
4. Any sentence where the word is used correctly.
   Examples:
   Heather found her dinner really **enjoyable**.
   Rachael did **remarkably** well in the bike race.
   The mountains became **visible** when the Sun came up.
   Anthony wrote more **legibly** after practising.
   The school was **accessible** for Ed's wheelchair.

Pages 84 and 85 — Suffixes

1. fam**ous**, angr**ily**, humor**ous**, scar**ily**
2. You should have ticked: **simplify** and **criticise**.
   You should have crossed: **justiceify**, **activeate**, **memoryise**, **terrorify**.
   The correct spellings are: **justify**, **activate**, **memorise**, **terrify**.
3. **advertise**, **decorate**, **summarise**, **classify**, **hyphenate**
4. author**ise**, origin**ate**, not**ify**, special**ise**, capital**ise**.
5. Any sentence where the word is used correctly.
   Examples:
   Dylan was able to sympath**ise** with Viv's situation.
   Seeing a skeleton is enough to horr**ify** anyone.
   I am still waiting for Gareth to apolog**ise**.

Section 15 — Confusing Words

Pages 86 and 87 — 'ei' and 'ie' Words

1. shr**ie**k, sh**ie**ld, f**ie**ld, w**ei**ght
2. c**ei**ling, pr**ie**st, rec**ei**ve, rel**ie**ve, gr**ie**f, bel**ie**ve, conc**ei**ve, dec**ei**ve.
3. You should have made: **piece**, **thief**, **chief**
4. **friend**, **relieved**, **seize**, **neighbour**

5. The answers to the clues are: **caffeine**, **receipt**, **thief**, **niece**, **brief**

```
T E I M N I E C E
M H R E I S I A E
H T I R E I W F F
I E S E A B N F L
U I E C F D E E I
E H I E E H E I G
I V T I E I T N I
L E O P O R E E R
E W S T H T I I E
E U B R I E F A I
```

Pages 88 and 89 — Words with 'ough' in

1. Words with 'ow' sound: **bough**, **plough**
   Words with 'or' sound: **fought**, **thought**, **sought**, **nought**
   Words with 'off' sound: **trough**, **cough**
2. **tough**, **enough**, **rough**
3. You should have linked: **bough** and **plough**, **borough** and **thorough**, **though** and **dough**, **brought** and **ought**.
4. **although**, **trough**, **nought**
5. **enough**, **ought**, **Throughout**, **tough**, **bought**
6. Any sentence where the word is used correctly.
   Examples:
   We went **through** the tunnel rather than over the mountain.
   Patrick was very **thorough** when checking for mistakes.
   I'm going to football practice even **though** I feel ill.

Pages 90 and 91 — Words with Silent Letters

1. ex**h**aust, **w**hen, **g**uess, **k**now, listen, **h**our, **k**nee, com**b**
2. is**l**and, lam**b**, **t**histle, si**g**n, ca**l**f, **g**host
3. Silent w words: s**w**ord, ans**w**er, **w**rite
   Silent h words: **wh**irl, **wh**eat, **wh**istle
   Silent g words: campai**g**n, **g**nome
   Silent b words: lim**b**, plum**b**er
4. **knocked**, **climbed**, **school**, **knife**, **honest**, **scent**
5. **Wednesday**, **often**, **debt**, **autumn**, **guess**
6. Any sentence where the word is used correctly.
   Examples:
   I was so hungry I ate everything — I didn't leave a **crumb**.
   It's time to **knuckle** down to some homework.
   Morris writes a **column** for a local newspaper.

Pages 92 and 93 — Unstressed Vowels

1. diff**e**rent, temp**e**rature, inter**e**sting, env**e**lope, eas**i**ly, pers**o**nal, inf**o**rmation, econ**o**mical, fright**e**ning, fatt**e**ning, off**e**ring, orig**i**nal
2. gen**e**ral, jew**e**llery, descr**i**be, bound**a**ry, pois**o**n, fam**i**ly, libr**a**ry
3. refrig**e**rate, confid**e**nt, veg**e**table, mem**o**ry, doct**o**r, concent**r**ate, bus**i**ness, marv**e**llous
4. Unstressed e: mis**e**rable, intellig**e**nce, desp**e**rate, deaf**e**ning
   Unstressed a: mini**a**ture, parli**a**ment, secret**a**ry, valu**a**ble
5. **dictionary**, **voluntary**, **literature**, **separate**

Answers

6. Any sentence where the word is used correctly.
   Examples:
   Jack was a very **generous** individual.
   Maya's **favourite** toy is a little giraffe.
   A badger is an **animal** that lives in the UK.

Pages 94 and 95 – Homophones

1. dessert, heel, mail, leek
2. **guest**, guessed, **father**, farther, **herd**, heard
3. night — **knight**, bawl — **ball**, beech — **beach**, daze — **days**, blue — **blew**, pane — **pain**, steel — **steal**

4. coarse (**course**), led (**lead**), lone (**loan**), worn (**warn**)
5. Any sentence where the word is used correctly.
   Examples:
   The train remained **stationary** for five minutes.
   I think you'll find a stapler in the **stationery** cupboard.
   The first point should **precede** the second.
   Let's **proceed** with the meeting.

Section 16 – Mixed Spelling Practice

Pages 96 to 98 – Mixed Spelling Practice

1. ach**ie**ve, rec**ei**pt, retr**ie**ve, hyg**ie**ne, misch**ie**f, cash**ie**r, perc**ei**ve, shr**ie**k
2. You should have ticked: **independent, emergency, intelligence, impossible**
   You should have crossed: **horrable, rodant, miserible, currancy, referance**
   The correct spellings are: **horrible, rodent, miserable, currency, reference**
3. Words with 'shul' ending: **influential, special, partial, artificial**
   Words with 'shun' ending: **technician, television, operation, fiction**
   Words with 'shus' ending: **gracious, ambitious, spacious, anxious**
4. You should have circled: rec**ie**ved, dou**g**t, m**ou**rning, rel**e**vent, **ke**y
   The correct spellings are: rec**ei**ved, dou**b**t, m**o**rning, rel**ev**ant, **qua**y
5. Words with 'uff' sound: **tough, rough, enough**
   Words with 'oh' sound: **although, though, dough**
   Words with 'or' sound: **sought, thought, nought**

6. ac**tive**, grace**ful**, simpl**ify**, electri**cian**, special**ise**
7. You should have made the words: **underwear, preview, enlarge, overload, midday, embolden, forename, nonsense**
   The hidden message is: **well done**
8. Any sentence where the words are used correctly.
   Examples:
   I decided I was going to **build** my new house myself.
   I'm sure the **rain** is more intense in the Lake District than elsewhere. OR I had to **rein** in my horse.
   I wore the **peak** of my cap down to hide my face.